Fitting
Your
Figure

from *Threads*

Fitting Your Figure

from **Threads**

The Taunton Press

Cover illustration: Glee Barre

Taunton
BOOKS & VIDEOS
for fellow enthusiasts

First printing: June 1994
Printed in the United States of America

A THREADS Book

THREADS® is a trademark of The Taunton Press, Inc.,
registered in the U.S. Patent and Trademark Office.

The Taunton Press
63 South Main Street
Box 5506
Newtown, CT 06470-5506

Library of Congress Cataloging-in-Publication Data

Fitting your figure / from Threads.
        p.   cm.
    "A Threads book" — T.p. verso
    Includes index.
    ISBN 1-56158-083-X
    1. Dressmaking—Pattern design. 2. Clothing and dress
    measurements. I. Threads magazine
TT520.F57   1994   94-4640
    646.4'072 — dc20   CIP

Contents

Introduction

as much as we might like to sew clothes, unless they fit, we're just spinning the wheels of our sewing machines. Let's face it: The necessity of understanding the shape of our bodies and that shape's relationship to a sewing pattern is an inescapable fact of sewing life. So here's an ideal package of information to help you face the facts: articles from *Threads* magazine on fit, pattern, clothes styling, adjustment and alterations.

In the following pages you'll learn how to take accurate measurements of yourself and your friends, and how to alter sewing patterns to reflect your body. You'll find a series of articles on padding and covering a dress form so it looks just like you. And if you need to grade a pattern to a size 2 or 22, the steps are described within. But we don't stop there. Experts offer tips about styling and details of specific clothing so you'll be confident that they're complementary—flattering skirt lengths, perfect shoulder shaping, just-right jackets.

So get out your tape measure, make a pot of coffee and invite over a friend. You're ready to make clothes that you enjoy wearing as well as sewing.

Amy T. Yanagi, editor

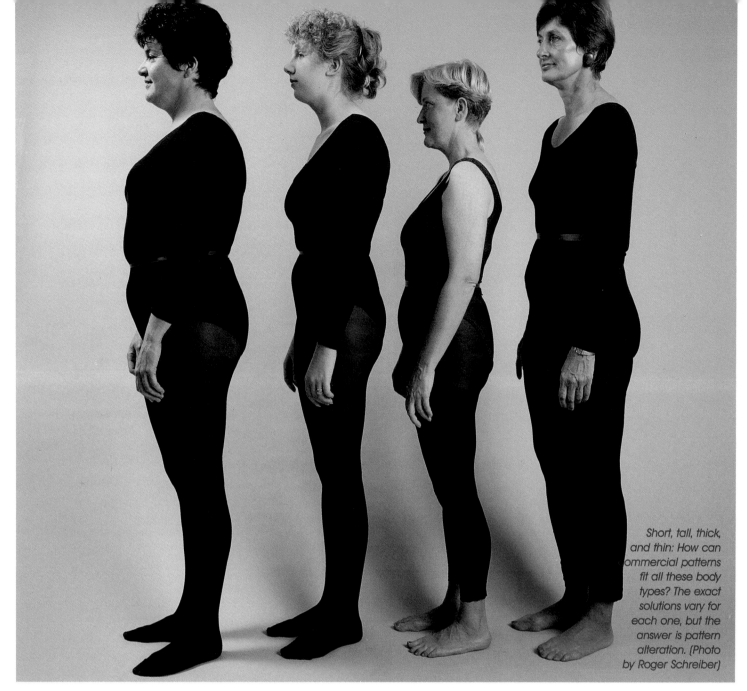

Short, tall, thick, and thin: How can commercial patterns fit all these body types? The exact solutions vary for each one, but the answer is pattern alteration. (Photo by Roger Schreiber)

Making Paper Patterns Fit Non-Paper Persons

Careful measurements make your garments measure up

by Dee DuMont

*a*h, the marvelous diversity of human bodies! These irregular cylinders come in such a wide variety of heights and distributions—long torso/short legs, short arms/wide back, full bust/small shoulders. The list is endless, and so are the fitting problems with a standard commercial pattern. Very few people can stitch up a given size right out of the envelope and have a perfect fit.

When a garment doesn't fit, you can sometimes alter it at the seamlines. You can make the pleat smaller, or nip in the hip. The curves of the breasts or the buttocks, though, do not usually occur at a seam. Fullness at the back of the neck or a protruding tummy appear in the center of many garment pieces. (One way to fit these body curves is through darting [see "Darting and alteration" on p. 13 for a discussion of darts].)

Although seamlines are really the only places you can alter an already-constructed piece of clothing, you can achieve a better fit by altering patterns within the silhouette of the garment. Alterations between the seamlines, while nearly impossible to make in cloth, are relatively easy to do on paper patterns.

How do you know whether you need to alter a pattern before you cut it out? When dealing with a new pattern, figure analysis and proper body measurement are the first steps in getting a pleasing fit. Begin with a careful look at your body, preferably in basic support garments but without fashion clothing. How is the body cylinder distributed? Where is the length? How do the body segments compare to each other? Where is the fullness? View yourself from all four sides, never bemoaning the uniqueness, just noting it.

Selecting a flattering style of clothing can reduce or even eliminate the need for an alteration. You can hide full thighs under a skirt that flares directly from the waist, for example. A full waistline may be less noticeable in a dropped-waist dress. (See *Threads*, No. 34, p. 44, for more on flattering styles.) But when you desire a fitted garment, with the look and style you see on the pattern envelope, you may have to alter the pattern.

Body measurement

The fit that results from measuring with careful attention to detail is well worth the time spent. While you need only four measurements (bust, waist, hip, and center back) to choose a commercial pattern size, 17 others provide data for specific body areas to help you decide when and where to change a pattern.

Before you begin measuring, you'll need to gather a few essential tools. The most important of these is a helper who will carefully locate reference points, wield a tape measure, and record the findings. You'll also need enough ribbon to go around your waist, a tape measure, and some firm string. You need a marking pen, and if you'll wear a leotard, a piece of chalk. Wear the basic undergarments you normally wear under clothing, unless you are planning a garment that requires a special bra, in which case it's important to measure wearing it.

The chart on the next page is a handy place to store the measurements you and your partner make. There are lines for the 21 body dimensions in column A. Columns B through E, coupled with a little basic math, help you locate problem areas in a pattern that you may want to alter. The numbered lines on the chart correspond to the numbers that are marked on the models in the photo at the top of page 11 and also on the pattern pieces in the drawing below it, allowing you to compare your measurements directly with those of the pattern. Once your personal facts are entered on the chart, use it as a semi-permanent reference tool for fitting, updating it periodically as necessary.

Your reference points—You'll need to mark several reference points before you begin measuring. Begin by tying a length of ribbon or firm string snugly around your *waistline*, confirming the location visually and verbally with your helper. Make certain that the string is parallel to the floor if possible.

Using a second piece of string, set up a simple *jewel neckline*. This line should be at the base of the neck just before the shoulders slope off, as shown in the left photo below. Use a pen to mark dots on the skin at the center front and center back on the jewel line.

With another string, mark the *sleeve seamline (armscye)* where the arm joins the shoulder. This need only be done on one side of the body, preferably the dominant side (i.e. right-handed, right side). The exception to this is if there is a major body variation, such as severe injury to one side of the body or if one side is significantly higher or larger than the other. In such cases, I recommend separate sets of measurements and pattern pieces for each quadrant of the body.

Mark the *shoulder point* with a short chalk line across the top of the armscye line following the string, as shown in the left-hand photo below.

Mark the *shoulder seamline* between the center front and center back, crossing the jewel neckline and the armscye seam, as shown in the right-hand photo below. Use a felt-tip pen to mark right on the skin, or mark a leotard with chalk. This should be done carefully, setting the line along the crest of the shoulder, neither too far forward nor too far back. Use your best judgement, and consult with your assistant as you both look in the mirror.

The measurements—There are a few simple rules that will allow the most accurate transfer of measurements from person to pattern: Make all circumference measurements carefully with the tape parallel to the floor. The three hipline points (3 in., 7 in., 9 in.; see drawing on p. 11) should be

 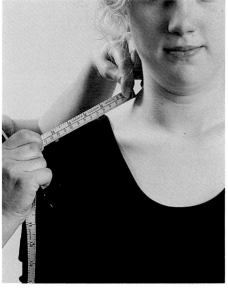

Reference points for measuring: The jewel neckline should fall near the dip between the collarbones in the front and at the base of the neck in back. The armscye line is positioned right where a perfectly fitted set-in sleeve would lie. Place the shoulder seam along the crest of the shoulder, neither too far forward nor too far back, and mark where it crosses the armscye line with chalk.

MEASUREMENT CHART (all measurements in inches)

Body area	A. Body measurements	B. Ease needed	C. Total A and B	D. Pattern measurement	E. Difference C and D Indicate (+) or (−)	F. Alter if E is greater than
1. Bust		2-3				1
2. Chest		N/A				1
3. Waist		1				1
4. Upper hip (3 in.)		1-2				1
5. Average hip (7 in.)		2-3				1
6. Lower hip (9 in.)		2-3				1
7. Center back (CB)		½				½
8. Neckrise		½				½
9. Diagonal back		½				½
10. Over shoulder blade		½				½
11. Upper back width		0				½
12. Shoulder length		0				¼
13. Center front (CF)		1				1
14. Bust point (BP) to CF neck		0				¼
15. BP to shoulder		0				¼
16. BP to BP		0				¼
17. BP to CF waist		½				½
18. Diagonal front		½				½
19. Over bust		½				½
20. Sleeve girth		3				2
21. Sleeve length		½				½

measured down from the waistline string along the side. If the fullest part of your hip is not 9 in. below your waist, measure the largest part and note the distance from the waistline on the chart.

During vertical measurements, like the center back, the tape should be held taut, falling the way actual cloth would fall, not necessarily following each curve and hollow of the body.

In addition to the obvious lengths you've set with string or see in the chart, there are a few areas that can be tricky to locate: Measure the *high bust*, or *chest*, around the torso with the tape going across the back at the bustline, but above the breasts in the front.

The *bust point* is the visual center of the breast, not necessarily the nipple point.

Measure *sleeve girth* around the arm at the base of the armscye with arm relaxed.

Sleeve length for women is measured from the shoulder point mark down to just below the prominent bone at the wrist.

Pattern selection
Use the bust, waist, 9-in. hip, and center-back measurements in column A of the measurement chart to select a commercial pattern size. Refer to the sizing page found in the back of most pattern catalogs to study the physical descriptions of the various sizing divisions, selecting the one closest to the measurements taken. If the

measurements fail to fall into a defined size range, choose a pattern that fits the torso and alter the waist and hips, since those are simpler alterations. If, however, the difference between the bust and chest measurements exceeds 2 in., select a pattern based on the waist, hip, and center back and alter for the bustline.

Sticking with the same pattern company over time increases pattern alteration success. Because a company usually uses the same master pattern for its styles, there is a certain consistency in fit. Even though all the American companies claim to use the same measurement standards, there is definitely a difference in the amount of basic ease allowed by the competing companies. Simplicity patterns are considerably more ample than Vogue. I usually refer my clients to Butterick, which provides the design excellence of Vogue, but is more readily available in my area and less expensive. I have recently worked with several New Look patterns. These have all sizes in each envelope, which is helpful when one's torso size is different from her pants or skirt size.

Column B on the measurement chart shows the minimum ease required to move in a woven-fabric garment. (Knit fabrics may not require as much ease because they stretch.) Add columns A and B and note the total in column C. This gives you the *minimum measurement* needed for each area of the body. When you are making a loosely

fitting style, the design of the fashion garment will undoubtedly provide more ease than the minimums listed in many areas, but there should not be less ease. Use your judgement. If the blouse has set-in sleeves, the upper back width and shoulder length measurements will still apply. But if you're making a jacket, it may be cut slightly larger across the back and shoulder seam to allow for a blouse or sweater to be worn underneath, and you would not want to reduce the pattern size to match the column C measurement because that would change the appearance of the garment. If the garment were a drop-shoulder style, it would be fruitless to attempt to correlate the shoulder seam measurements.

Should you alter?
When you have your measurements, you need to measure the pattern and compare its measurements to yours. Seam allowances, darts, and pleats are not part of the final garment measurement, so you must remember to exclude them during measuring. Measure from seamline to seamline, not across seam allowances or darts. Add the measurements together for the total. Beginning with the bust, measure the bodice front at the level of your bust point to center front. The bust point is below the bottom of the armscye for regular patterns, but may not be on a raglan or deep-armhole sleeve. If there's a question,

use measurement 14, the bust point to CF neck, and measurement 15 to find your line. Double the bodice front distance, then measure the bodice back. Double that and add the front and back together. This is the actual pattern measurement to be entered in column D of the chart.

Measure the waist of both the pattern front and back at the marked waistline, and the hip measurements 3, 7, and 9 in. below that. Remember not to include the center area of any darts or pleats. Add the front and back measurements, multiply by two, and write the total in the appropriate boxes in column D.

Continue through the chart, measuring as closely as possible to the lines illustrated on the sloper pattern at right.

Note that a pattern need not be a sloper style in order to find the reference lines. You can easily measure a princess style by pinning the center front and side front together at the point through which you're measuring.

Now compare the column C numbers with column D. For example, the bust measurement with ease added in column C is 42 in., and the pattern measures only 37½ in. Since column F says to alter the bust if the difference between C and D is 1 in. or more, you would add at least 4½ in. to the pattern, depending on the style ease required.

If you've decided to alter

When the measurement chart and personal judgement show you need a pattern alteration, a few basic tools are in order. I prefer sharp pencils over felt-tip pens, because they're more accurate. You'll need a good ruler and a T-square, but a clear plastic ruler with ⅛-in. cross markings can do both jobs. A good yardstick is essential, not the free-at-the-paint-store variety. I use a metal one. A french curve, available at most notion counters, is useful in truing curves. A toothed tracing wheel for perforating pattern markings; clear tape that you can write on, like Scotch Magic Tape; and tissue paper for filler (the unfolded kind on rolls doesn't require ironing) complete the necessary supplies.

Pattern alterations are best made either parallel or perpendicular to the grainlines. This minimizes the potential for distorting the pattern pieces and provides a basic organization for the alteration process.

The most basic rule for pattern alteration is that the pattern must remain flat. Most alterations are made by slashing the pattern and then either spreading it apart to increase the size or overlapping the sections to decrease the size. A slash can be all the way through the pattern; or to, but not through, a given point, leaving a tiny piece of paper uncut. In the latter case, the slash stops at a specified place called a pivot point, around

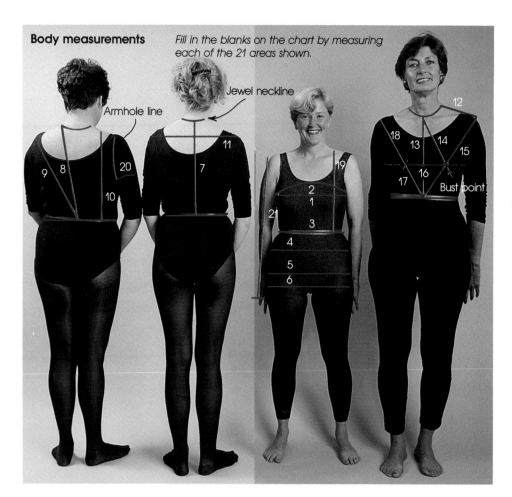

Body measurements *Fill in the blanks on the chart by measuring each of the 21 areas shown.*

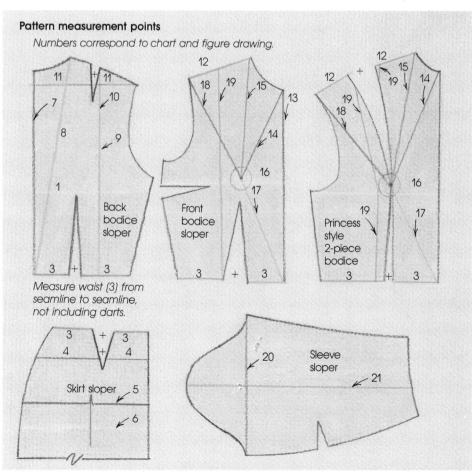

Pattern measurement points
Numbers correspond to chart and figure drawing.

Back bodice sloper

Front bodice sloper

Princess style 2-piece bodice

Measure waist (3) from seamline to seamline, not including darts.

Skirt sloper

Sleeve sloper

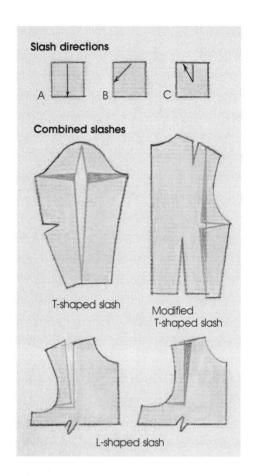

Slash directions

A B C

Combined slashes

T-shaped slash

Modified
T-shaped slash

L-shaped slash

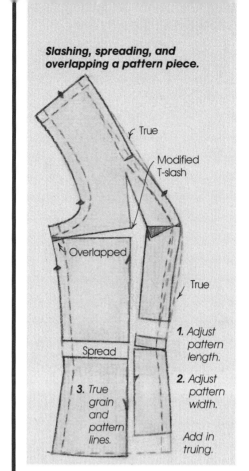

Slashing, spreading, and overlapping a pattern piece.

True

Modified
T-slash

Overlapped

True

1. Adjust pattern length.

Spread

2. Adjust pattern width.

3. True grain and pattern lines.

Add in truing.

The fitted muslin (above): *After pattern alteration, last-minute adjustments can often be made along existing seamlines. This muslin fits well and won't need many changes.*

The finished blouse (at right): *Well fitted, with enough ease, but not too much, the custom blouse is the result of careful pattern alteration.*

which the two pieces of the pattern will then move as they are spread or overlapped. It is impossible to cut into the middle of a piece of paper, spread the two sides apart or overlap them, and have the paper remain flat. Any slash must go to two sides of the paper. As indicated in the drawing above, slashes can go to **A**, opposite sides; **B**, adjacent sides; or even to **C**, the same side; but in each case the paper will remain flat when the process is complete.

Slashes can also be combined to form a T-shape, a modified T, or an L-shape. A T-shaped slash that goes to, but not through, all four end points is used when increasing the girth of a sleeve. A modified T can be used to decrease fullness in the bodice back when the slash begins at the waistline and goes to, but not through, both the shoulder and the underarm. An L-shaped slash originating at the shoulder seam and terminating at the notch point on the armscye can be used to adjust the length of the shoulder seam.

The slashed pattern can be spread or overlapped evenly or unevenly. When the pattern is spread, tissue paper is used as filler and taped to the altered pattern. You might spread evenly when lengthening a sleeve pattern, or unevenly when the center back requires lengthening but the front does not. In the latter case, you would slash from center back to, but not through, the side seam, and spread to increase the length at center

back, without changing the front.

When adjusting circumference measurements, you will usually divide the amount to be altered by four to disperse it evenly, one-quarter of the amount going into each quarter of the garment. For example, if the waistline requires a 1-in. increase, ½ in. would go across the whole front and ½ in. across the whole back. Since a simple skirt, for example, has only two pieces—the front and back—the amount of increase on each pattern piece would be just ¼ in.

An alteration for a specific area such as a large bust is an exception. Usually, the full increase is made on the front pattern piece. However, if a bust measurement indicates the need for an alteration, but the bust is not unusually large when compared to the high bust, the amount to be added could be dispersed on both the front and back pattern pieces. If the body is quite wide across the back and fairly average in the front, the spread might be required only on the back pattern piece. Similar situations can arise in every area of the figure, and careful body analysis and experience will determine the proper location for an alteration.

Limitations and exceptions—Your alterations should not cause a serious distortion of the pattern. Generally, an increase or decrease of no more than ½ in. per slash is acceptable. If more is needed, you can usually make an additional slash nearby

and repeat the process. This ensures a gradual change in the pattern piece, resulting in a smooth, even appearance, with the basic design and silhouette of the garment unchanged. But sometimes you need to break the rules as when you need to increase the bust measurement over 4 in. across the front or when you need to lengthen pattern pieces.

Finishing up—Pattern alterations that change seam lengths must occur in corresponding places on adjacent pattern pieces. If the side seam of the bodice front is increased, the side seam of the adjoining piece, the bodice back, must also be increased because eventually these two pieces will be sewn together. Further, the adjacent alterations must originate from the same place on both pieces, for example, 3 in. up from the waistline seam. After each alteration, ask yourself, "to what other pattern piece will this one be sewn?" and alter the adjoining pattern if necessary.

When you've finished altering the pattern, it must be trued. All distorted or changed lines are returned to their original character (not to their original size). If the seamline was straight before the alteration, it must remain straight; if it was originally curved, it must be similarly curved. Truing should be done from seam intersection to seam intersection, using your ruler, yardstick, or a french curve to make a clean,

Darting and alteration

Darts play a major role in making an orginally flat piece of fabric fit a three-dimensional person. Changing their size, angle, or location can make a big difference in how a garment fits. Dart length is the distance from the tip of the dart, to the seam from which it originates. Dart size is the angle at which the two sides intersect; it determines the fit more than any other factor. The larger the angle, the more fabric will be used to fit over the protrusion. The most common uses of the dart are at the waistline of pants and skirts, for waist fitting in jackets, and, of course, in fitting over the bust.

To position the bust dart properly, first locate the wearer's actual bust point on the bodice front, by using measurements 13 through 16 in column C of the chart on p. 10 and transferring them to the pattern. Then draw a bust circle on the pattern as reference. This loosely represents the mass of the breast. For sizes up to 12, the diameter of this bust circle is 3 in. For larger sizes, the diameter is 4 in. to 5 in. The bust circle determines the dart length; dart tip must extend at least to the outer edge of the circle so the fullness it releases will fall over the fullest part of the bust. The closer the tip extends toward the bust point, the more defined the bust will be, creating a sharper, less rounded appearance.

If the pattern already has a dart, you can find the bust point by bisecting the dart as shown in the top left drawing below and extending the line through the dart tip. In sizes 12 and under, the bust point should be approximately 1½ in. from the tip; in larger sizes, from 2 to 2½ in. from the tip. If it's not where it should be, move it as shown in the right drawing below.

Darts can also "hide" in seamlines, as in the princess style. Princess lines run across the center of the bust parallel with the center front, beginning from either the shoulder seam or the armscye and ending at the waist or hem. You can see the dartlike aspect of princess line seams when the front and side pattern pieces are placed next to each other with seamlines lapped at the bust point, as shown in the bottom left drawing. The darting here comes from the shoulder and waistline seams, rather than side and waist as in a sloper. Princess seams are flattering to every bust size because they allow custom adjustments for a smooth transition from the upper chest area over the bust and down to the waist. —D.D.

definite line between them. For example, if you lengthen the bodice front below the dart, place your ruler at the bottom of the dart and the intersection of the side seam and waist seam. Draw a straight line. True the center front between the neckline seam and the waist seam. Remember to reestablish cutting lines and seam allowances (see drawing on facing page). Seamlines which will be sewn together must be the same length, including the two sides of a dart, so be sure to check and make adjustments while you are truing. After you true the seamlines, true the cutting lines parallel to them.

If the pattern is complicated, or if you've made many changes, you might want to cut a muslin to confirm your work, before you cut the fashion fabric. Sometimes another set of pattern alterations is needed, and sometimes only slight adjustments to the muslin will bring you to the finished look.

The muslin in the photo on the facing page shows the result of the alteration from the measurement chart to the flat pattern. The completed custom-fit blouse (photo, above) justifies the time spent measuring. □

Dee DuMont is a custom seamstress, designer, and pattern-making instructor in the Pacific Northwest. She was a wardrobe seamstress for the filming of An Officer and A Gentleman *in Port Townsend, WA. (All photos by Roger Schreiber)*

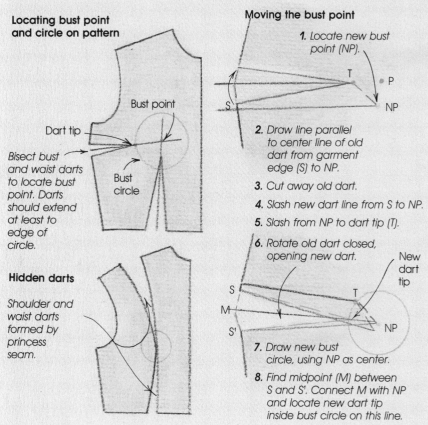

Locating bust point and circle on pattern

Dart tip

Bust point

Bisect bust and waist darts to locate bust point. Darts should extend at least to edge of circle.

Bust circle

Hidden darts

Shoulder and waist darts formed by princess seam.

Moving the bust point

1. Locate new bust point (NP).

T   P   NP   S

2. Draw line parallel to center line of old dart from garment edge (S) to NP.

3. Cut away old dart.

4. Slash new dart line from S to NP.

5. Slash from NP to dart tip (T).

6. Rotate old dart closed, opening new dart.

New dart tip

S   M   S¹   T   NP

7. Draw new bust circle, using NP as center.

8. Find midpoint (M) between S and S¹. Connect M with NP and locate new dart tip inside bust circle on this line.

Measuring Yourself When You're Home Alone

Tools and tips for working without an assistant

by Britta Callamaras

no doubt you've been told that it's impossible to measure yourself accurately. Not true! With a little ingenuity, you can make a detailed and reliable analysis of your own figure. With these measurements, you can solve fitting and pattern-adjusting problems or draft new basic and fashion or knitting patterns, using any method you prefer. Once you assemble the tools I recommend, they can help make fitting yourself easier, as well.

The problem with measuring yourself is how to do it without distorting your normal stance while you move the tape measure around. My method depends on three simple ideas that together eliminate the problem. First, I use two modified mirrors so I can easily see my entire figure from the front, sides, or back without twisting. I also use colored tape and adhesive dots—along with safety pins and rubber bands—to make clearly visible, secure markings on my skin and undergarments. Finally, I've devised simple methods for holding and adjusting the measuring tape so I don't shift my arms and shoulders any more than necessary when taking measurements.

The specific measurements I'll describe include all the ones I use to draft fitting basics (or slopers) for bodices and skirts, plus a few unusual ones that have helped me unravel knotty fitting puzzles. If I've overlooked measurements that you need, perhaps you can use my methods to take these, too.

Supplies

Here's a list of essential equipment:

Mirrors—You'll need one full-length mirror. It should be large enough to see your entire length and width when you're standing about 3 or 4 ft. away, close enough to read the reflected numbers on your measuring tape when the tape's against your body. This mirror doesn't have to be permanently wall mounted, but it should be leaning very close to vertical against the wall when you use it.

For viewing my back in the large mirror, I use a small (6- to 8-in. diameter) nonenlarging mirror attached to a stand so that it's at my eye level, and easy to move around; I'm using it in the photo on the facing page. I asked a carpenter friend to build a simple stand with wheels. It's ideal, but anything that keeps your mirror steady, high enough, and nearly parallel to the large mirror is fine. Perhaps you could tape or wire your mirror to an easel, a tripod, or a step ladder.

On the face of the full-length mirror, I tape reference lines using 1/4-in. colored tape (described below). One line is vertical and two are horizontal, positioned at about the level of my hip and bust, when I'm in viewing position; you can put in more lines if you like. I use a plumb line (a long string with a weight at one end) to check the vertical, and I check the horizontals by measuring each end from the top of the mirror; you could also use a carpenters' level. With these lines in place, I can now visually confirm that all the horizontal and vertical measurements I take *are* horizontal or vertical.

Marking tools—To make everything as clear and easy to see as possible, I mark directly on my figure all the points and lines I need to measure between. The marks need to be bold, nonshifting, nonsmearing, and permanent until I'm done with them. Safety pins work perfectly to establish hip levels on my slip, and rubber bands are handy for marking wrist and arm, but I rely on pressure-sensitive graphic tape and adhesive dots for other areas. The ink-based markers I've used on my skin always smeared or wore off before I was finished.

Graphic tape is available inexpensively at art supply stores and comes in many bright colors and widths from 1/64 in. up. I use the 1/8-in. width for marking on my body, and the 1/4-in. tape for marking the mirror. I used to use masking tape, but it didn't stick to my skin as well, didn't show up on my skin, and was too wide to be precise. Also available are colored adhesive dots that are ideal for marking points like shoulders.

To mark my waistline, I make a fitting band from a strip of fabric folded and stitched to a finished width of 1 in., and long enough to fit comfortably around my waist. On one end I put a couple of hooks, which I fasten to small safety pins on the other end so the band can be adjusted precisely. When I'm measuring to or from my waistline, I always measure to the bottom of the band. I also use the band when draping or fitting skirts and pants (see *Threads* No. 38, p. 8).

To mark perfectly vertical side seams, I make two plumb lines from lengths of narrow ribbon with small weights at one end (I use washers, nuts, or fishing weights). At the other end I put snaps so the ribbons can be secured in place over the waistband. Once snapped to the band, I anchor each ribbon near the hip with a short length of tape, as you can see in the photo on the facing page.

I also buy enough 1-in.-wide elastic to fit around my chest. It angles up in front, fitting above the bust, but I make it level in back as a reference line for measuring vertically to the shoulder and neckline. Because it fits snugly up under my armpits, its lower edge coincides with the bottom of the armscye, 1 in. below the arm/body joint.

I establish my neckline with a short necklace, or a length of plain keychain or lamp pullchain (the kind made from little balls and linked together with a snap that holds two balls together) from the

From *Threads* magazine (April 1992) 40:60-65

Britta Callamaras takes her own measurements accurately with the help of reference lines marked on a full-length mirror, plumb lines at her sides to establish side seams, and important reference lines marked on her body with colored tape.

hardware store. Once it's adjusted to fall where I'd like my neckline, I mark around the chain with graphic tape, as you can see in the photo at right, because the tape won't shift.

Measuring aids—The most basic tool you'll need is a tape measure with large, easy-to-read numerals. I use the small hole at the "No. 1 end" (my term for the beginning of the tape—"tail end" means the rest of it) to attach a weight to it. You'll see why below.

An odd piece of equipment you'll need is an underarm level, shown in the photo on p. 17. It's made from a piece of cardboard about 8 by 11 in. Draw a straight line parallel to, and about an inch away from, each short end. Make two 1-ft. plumb lines from weights and string and attach them to one long edge of the cardboard so they hang down right on top of the lines. You'll put this underarm level snug up under your arm. When the strings fall parallel to the lines, the top edge will be horizontal and at the level of your underarm, making several different shoulder and armscye measurements easier to take.

Marking your body

Before you measure yourself, you need to find and mark on your body all the key places from which to measure: hips, waistline, neckline, shoulders, armscyes, wrists, etc. People are asymmetrical, so be sure to mark and measure both sides of yourself.

Finding the "right" place to mark involves at least as much personal preference as physiology. You're the final judge of what looks good to you and how you want your clothes to fit, so I recommend you regard the following descriptions as starting points for your own decisions.

Hips and waist—Wear your usual undergarments and shoes in your usual heel height. Fasten your waistband (line A in drawing 1 on p. 16) so it's neither tight nor loose. If it goes up over the tummy, you can loosen the belting a little, but if it's too loose, you won't get accurate measurements. Don't try to get your waistline horizontal if it isn't naturally.

Fasten the two ribbon plumb lines over the waistband and slide them around to

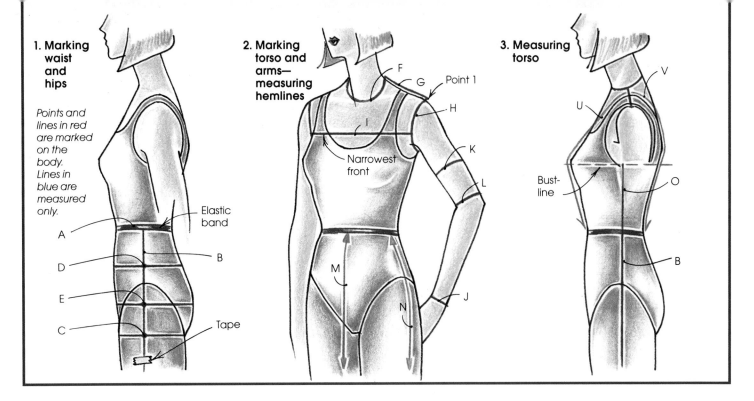

1. Marking waist and hips

Points and lines in red are marked on the body. Lines in blue are measured only.

Elastic band

A
D
E
C
B
Tape

2. Marking torso and arms— measuring hemlines

F
G
Point 1
H
I
Narrowest front
K
L
M
N
J

3. Measuring torso

V
U
Bust-line
O
B

---

the sides so they divide the body in half vertically (line B, drawing 1 above), choosing the most flattering division between front and back. Usually the front waistline is an inch longer than the back, but choose whatever looks best to you. Tape down the ribbons below the hip level to keep them secure.

The hipline (C) is the circumference at the point where your hips are widest as seen from the front. If your hip bones protrude near the waistline in front, measure there, too, as a high hipline. Pin a safety pin on each near the ribbon at each point. I also check the side views to mark the most prominent points at the tummy (D) and derriere (E), hip bone, and thigh. I place pins along the ribbon at these points, too, using the horizontal reference lines in the mirror to make sure I'm transferring them accurately to the side.

Neckline—To identify your neckline (F, drawing 2 above), make a necklace from your chain, adjusting it until it falls where you like. A high round neckline usually sits ¼ in. to ½ in. below the necklace in front, but coincides with the necklace line at the back of the neck. Neckline/collar seams should also match the necklace shape in back. I feel uncomfortable if a garment edge touches the hollow between my collar bones, so I put a short piece of graphic tape horizontally just below it. This marks the highest comfortable neckline, or neckline seam, for me; yours may be different.

Holding one end of your graphic tape in one hand and the container in the other, pull out several inches, and reach up and

over the head so you can pull the tape to the back of your neck to lie right under the necklace. Cut the tape and complete the front neckline by positioning graphic tape along the necklace in front, incorporating the line you used to mark your highest comfortable neckline. Stand back to see if it looks round, and adjust until you are pleased. The bottom third should be horizontal and straight.

Shoulders—Where do your shoulders end and your arms start? To find the shape of your armscye, you must find both the shoulder point and the arm joint. Usually, you can see a short wrinkle where your arm joins your body at the armpit in front. If you follow that line up to the place on the top of your shoulder that feels like a little seam or crack when you raise your arm, you will have traveled up the joint line.

That crack at the top plane of your shoulder marks the end of your shoulder and the start of your arm. The bump you can feel as you move away from your neck when your arm is down is where your shoulder bones end. This is where most directions tell you to mark your shoulder point.

With a stick-on dot, mark both shoulders at the shoulder point (point 1, same drawing) at the outer edge of the bump. Now you need to make some choices, carefully considering what you think looks best on you and what sort of garments you like to make.

For example, for knits or gathered sleeves, you may wish to measure your shoulder line from the necklace to the

crack on top. For woven fabrics, perhaps a measurement to the bump will look best, and for suits and padded shoulders, you'll measure out to the outer edge of the arm.

Now, standing sideways to the big mirror, look along your shoulder to your ear, using your small mirror so that your neck isn't turned. Imagine a dot about an inch behind the ear. Ideally, you could draw a straight line from the ear dot to the shoulder point dot, and this would be your shoulder line (line G). If you were fortunate, this line would not show from either the front or back when you turned to face the mirror.

This ideal line would also not swing towards the front or back when seen from above. What if yours does, or for any other reason you don't like your first line? Move it. Move the shoulder dot, and the graphic tape line, to the most becoming place, in your opinion, as close to the ideal as possible. Don't worry if your line doesn't bisect the arm equally from the side view, but try to position your line on the apex of the shoulder mass, so that no part of it is clearly visible from the front or the back. A well-placed shoulder line is so important to the appearance of your garments that it's worth being very precise and fussy over.

Armscyes—Finding your sleeve/bodice seam placement (your armscye, line H) is easy if you take a large rubber band and slip it over your arm and up to the joint of your arm and shoulder. It should fit your armpit comfortably. Adjust it so it lies on your chosen shoulder point and also right on top of the armpit wrinkle described earlier. Tape the band in place at the shoulder, and in front, especially if it needs to curve inward to follow your contours. In a traditional fitted garment, that is where the armscye seam would lie, dipping to about 1 in. below the armpit at the bottom. In a suit, the seam would be moved out past the shoulder point so the sleeve could hang straight down from it. Shoulder pads would be used to fill up the excess space.

For measuring, mark the line with graphic tape. In front, just pull the tape from the shoulder point down the line of the band to the top of the wrinkle. The line may curve a little or a lot.

To do the back easily by yourself, pull out about 1 ft. of tape and dangle the dispenser box from it, in the hand opposite the shoulder you're marking. Looking in your small mirror at your reflection in the large one, hang the tape over the rubber band in back, and press the tape to your shoulder point on the back side so it is securely fastened at the top of the shoulder. Keep the arm being marked relaxed and hanging naturally. Let go of the tape and, reaching under the armpit, pull the tape close to the body into the armscye line. Since your hanging arm will be forward to do this, the tape will automatically mark the widest part of your back and end at the wrinkle of the back armpit. This line is usually straighter than the one in front but may slant or curve out at the bottom. When it's marked to the start of the armpit, cut the tape from the box.

Returning to the front, mark your "narrowest front" (line I). This is where your armscyes curve in toward your chest. When you have found the narrowest place between them, use a horizontal line of graphic tape from side to side to show where it is.

I establish landmarks on my arms with more rubber bands. The lines to mark are the wrists (J), the largest place (usually your biceps, K), and where you'd like your short sleeves to end (L). There's usually no need to mark the elbows.

Taking measurements

Now that you're all marked, you can start to measure yourself. In order to ensure accurate measurements, I never look down at the tape to read the numbers; I read the tape in the mirror. It's not too hard to read the backwards numbers, and if I look in the small mirror, the reflections are the right way around again. I've also learned to pinch the tape to mark the point I want to read after I've moved it.

Waist and hips—A skirt or pair of pants must be as big as your front in the front and as big as your back in back if they are to hang straight. But you need more than just the total circumference. The front and back must be measured separately at their widest parts, starting and ending at the side seam ribbons.

At the level of one safety pin marker, place the No. 1 end of the tape at one side seam, and the tail at the other side seam. Without looking down, compare the level of the tape with the horizontal line on the mirror to be sure you're holding the tape level. Pinch the tape on the tail end and bring it to the front to read the number. Repeat for all of the pinned levels, front and back. Then record the distance each level is from the waistband.

To measure the length of the curves between waist and hips, use a tape measure with a weight on the No. 1 end. Suspend it so the end is at the floor, so you can use this measurement to mark even, level hemlines. Record the measurement from the floor to the bottom of the waistband (lines M and N, drawing 2 on the facing page). Do this at the center front and back, then left and right sides. To find the skirt length, subtract the inches from the floor you want your hemline to be from each of the above measurements. The result will be the length of the material required for that area. Now you can put the skirt on the ironing board, measure those places from the completed waistband, taper the measurements between them, and mark an even hemline.

Upper torso—The bust measurement should also be taken separately for front and back. First find the side seams at the underarm (line O, drawing 3 on the facing page); they should line up with the skirt side seams. Hold the weighted tape measure as a plumb line to extend the lines. When it's correctly placed, hold it there with the arm it's under, and with the other hand, stick on a dot at the level of the fullest bust next to the tape measure. You'll be able to feel the dot, or see it in the mirror, when you measure the bustline front and back from side to side. Check the levels in the big mirror. You can raise both hands to hold the tape ends as long as you remember to relax your shoulders and arms when you pinch the tape to take the actual measurement. You may also want a bust point-to-point measurement, taken at the same level. If you have prominent shoulder blades, record the most prominent parts, and the distance between them, as described below.

Above the armscye, horizontal mea-

surements obviously stop at the armscye. In front you'll need the narrowest front (I), which establishes the distance from armscye to armscye on fitted garments. In back, I measure horizontally from shoulder point to point (line P, drawing 4, p. 18). and across the shoulder blades between the armscyes at mid-armscye (Q), checking levels in the mirror. To hold the tape, I use the bath-towel-across-your-back technique, as I'm doing in the photo on p. 15.

Paint one leg of a large paper clip with red nail polish, as a marker on the tape measure. Slide the red leg on top of the 10- or 20-in. mark, depending on your size. Pretend that the marked spot is the 1-in. mark on the tape, and you will then have a handle on the tape to hold in one hand while the other hand pulls the marker to the marked place on the body. You can also tie a string through the hole at the No. 1 end. Read the measurement number in the mirror, and subtract the 10 or 20 inches that you started with.

Measure your neckline by following the line of tape around the necklace. Record the back width between shoulder lines, and the circumference.

Shoulders—To measure your shoulder line, pull the No. 1 end of the tape over the marked line from the dot towards your neckline, and read the measurement at the dot. Record any other shoulder lengths you want there, as well.

To find the shape of your shoulders and

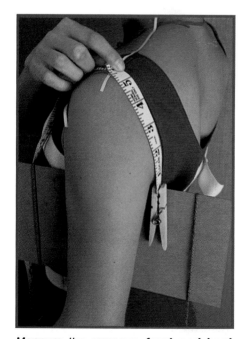

*Measure the **armscye front and back** from shoulder dot to underarm level. Throw the weighted end of the tape over your shoulder and look in the mirror to see when it hits the top of the level.*

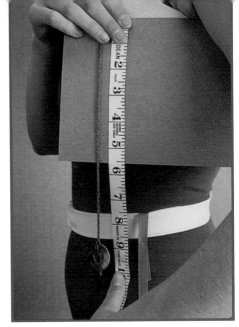 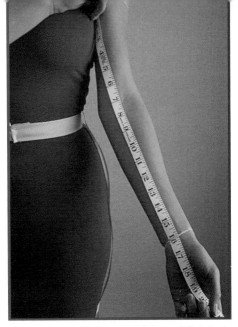

Measure your **underarm side-seam length** *(above left) from the waist tape (slightly in front of the actual seam) to the top of the underarm level.*

To measure your **underarm length** *(above right), pull the tape measure through the rubber band on your wrist and up to a band positioned 1 in. below your armpit.*

The **top of the sleeve cap** *(below) should be measured if your shoulder protrudes in front. Tape the starting end of your tape measure to the armscye line in back and pull it horizontally to the front armscye line.*

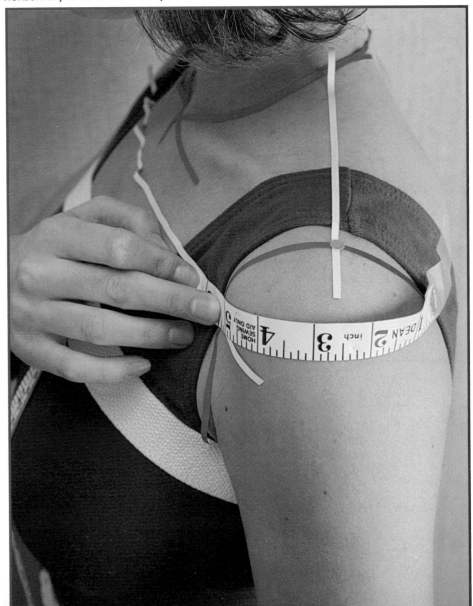

length of your back, first pin a length of 1-in.-wide elastic around your chest at the armpit level, and check that the back is level. Dangle the weighted end of the tape over your shoulder so it can measure vertically from the bottom of the elastic to points along the shoulder line (drawing 4 below). Measure both sides along the armscye at the narrowest point (R), and at the points where the shoulder lines and neckline meet (S), and at CB. When the tape is in place, pinch it at the shoulder line.

To measure the full CB length (T), hold the No. 1 end of the tape at the waistband with one hand, the tail end with the other at the necklace, and pinch. Also measure vertically from the midshoulders to the waistband, **over the bust points in front (U, drawing 3, p. 16)**, and in **back (V)**.

Measure the front shoulder shape with vertical measurements up from the horizontal line across the narrowest front. Measure at the **center front (W, drawing 5, facing page)**, at the **neckline/shoulder line junction (X)**, and at the **ends of the horizontal line (Y)**.

Armscyes—To measure around your armscye, drape the tape over your shoulder with the tail in back and the No. 1 end any place along the armscye. With the other hand, reach under your armpit to grab the tail of the tape, then use the opposite hand to tighten the circle until it's snug but not tight. Pinch it so you can drop the No. 1 end.

To find the true armhole depth, it is necessary to use several different measurements together. One of these is the

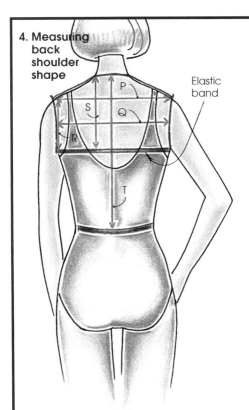

4. Measuring back shoulder shape

Elastic band

side-seam length (Z). To find it, put your cardboard level under your arm and adjust so that the strings coincide with the drawn lines, then hold it in place with that arm. With that same hand, hold the No. 1 end of the tape measure even with the bottom edge of your waistband. With the other hand bring the tape up vertically (a little in front of your actual side seam) to the top of the cardboard and read the measurement in the mirror, as in the top left photo on the facing page.

The next measurements, which measure how much of your armscye is in the front and in back of your shoulder point, are taken from the shoulder point down to the level cardboard. Take a separate measurement for the front armscye (AA) (drawing 6, below) and back (BB) for each arm, holding your shoulders in a natural, relaxed position. To measure the fronts, weight the No. 1 end of your tape, and throw the tail of the tape over your shoulder. With the opposite hand, inch up the tape so that the No. 1 end touches the top of the cardboard and your hand can feel when you touch the shoulder-point dot. Pinch the tape and bring it to the front to read. To do the backs, throw the weighted end over your shoulder and check in the mirror to see when it touches the cardboard, as in the photo on p. 17.

You will have to remember that all measurements to the top of the underarm level need to be adjusted to reflect the bottom of the armscye 1 in. below it, adding an inch for measurements starting above the level, and subtracting for measurements from below.

I always find it very useful to know the width of the armhole (CC, drawing 6, below). To measure it, use a strip of paper folded in half the long way. Near one end of the folded edge, make a dark vertical line. With the folded edge uppermost, put the paper under your arm, checking the horizontal against the lines in the mirror. Standing so you can see your side in the mirror, pull the paper to the front until the line at the back touches the back edge of your arm, then mark the front edge of the arm. Repeat for the other arm. The bottom halves of your armholes need to be at least this distance from front to back when your pattern is joined at the side seam, and not much more.

Arms—I measure the wrist first because it's easiest, but all the circumferences are managed the same way. I just throw the tape over my arm, retaining the No. 1 end in my other hand. With both ends of the tape in this hand, I manipulate the tape until the No. 1 end is where I can see it, looking down. I press the No. 1 end to the arm with one finger while I pull the tape snug with the others.

However you do it, move this circle of tape to the next place you want to measure. On your wrist, it is over the bump on the outer side of your arm. On the elbow, it is with the elbow bent. When measuring the biceps, flatten your arm against your side to expand it, and check that the tape is level.

To measure length on the arms (DD, drawing 7, below), use the rubber band marker at the wrist to hold the tail of the tape while you pull the other end up to your shoulder point. To measure to the el-bow or the entire arm length, maneuver the tape so it will go under the band on the back of the hand side and over your slightly bent elbow while you hold the other end in the hand of the arm being measured. To find the elbow-to-shoulder length, measure from wrist to elbow and subtract from the total length.

To measure the sleeve underarm length (EE), shift the tape to the palm side of the wristband. Move the rubber band that's around the biceps up the arm until it's 1 in. below the armpit, using a 1-in.-wide ruler to determine that point. This establishes the bottom of the arm-scye; measure to the band, as in the top right photo on the facing page.

For the sleeve cap length (FF), make sure the rubber band just described is level, then measure from the shoulder point to the band along the outside of the arm. If you've got a prominent, forward-facing shoulder bone, measure how far down from the shoulder point the prominence is. Then measure horizontally across the arm to find the sleeve cap width (GG) you need there. Tape the No. 1 end of the measuring tape to the back armscye along that horizontal line, as in the bottom photo on the facing page, and measure across to the front seamline. If you want a short sleeve length, slip the underarm level under your arm and measure down from its top edge to where you want the sleeve to end. □

Britta Callamaras is an avid teacher of sewing and machine knitting. She is a frequent contributor to the Fitting *column in* Threads *magazine.*

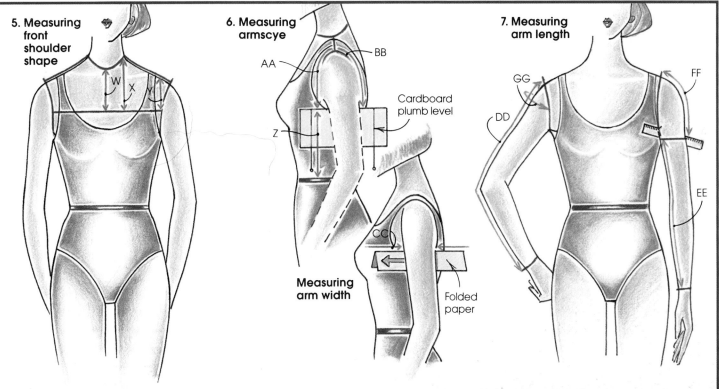

5. Measuring front shoulder shape

W X Y

6. Measuring armscye

AA
BB
Z
Cardboard plumb level
CC
Measuring arm width
Folded paper

7. Measuring arm length

GG
DD
FF
EE

Illustrations by Pierre Poulard

Pattern Alteration Made Easy

Pivot and slide to a better fit

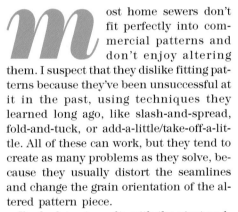

*by Nancy Zieman
with Robbie Fanning*

most home sewers don't fit perfectly into commercial patterns and don't enjoy altering them. I suspect that they dislike fitting patterns because they've been unsuccessful at it in the past, using techniques they learned long ago, like slash-and-spread, fold-and-tuck, or add-a-little/take-off-a-little. All of these can work, but they tend to create as many problems as they solve, because they usually distort the seamlines and change the grain orientation of the altered pattern piece.

I've had great results with the pivot-and-slide method of altering patterns, shown in the photo above, which creates none of these problems. It's a simple, comparatively fast, and effective method of repositioning the seamlines without disturbing the original pattern. As a result, the grainline isn't altered, and seamline changes are always in proportion to the original pattern. You can even make subtle adjustment to finished or basted garments (see "Fine-tuning with pivot and slide" on p. 23).

We'll be changing pattern width by pivoting, and pattern length by sliding. All alterations are made on a worksheet (I like to use wax paper, but you can also use tissue paper, or a non-woven fabric like Pellon's Tru-Grid), which keeps the original pattern unchanged. The only other tools you'll need are standard sewing room equipment: pins, fine-point permanent marking pens in red

and black, a ruler, a tracing wheel, transparent tape, and a tape measure.

Start with classic shapes

You can alter any pattern with pivot-and-slide, but it's easiest to learn on a classic-style blouse, skirt, dress, or jacket. In fact, once you know what alterations you need on a classic-style pattern, you can automatically make those same changes on every pattern from that company, no matter what the style.

By classic, I mean patterns with set-in sleeves and no dropped shoulders; shoulder seams, with no yoke over the shoulders (a decorative front or back yoke is fine); no excessive gathering, tucking, or pleating on the sleeves or body; not oversized; and straight, A-line, or bias-cut skirts without excessive fullness. Once you can pivot and slide classic styles, you'll be able to alter any style, including highly detailed or extremely oversized or formfitting styles.

Classic pattern styles are available in ev-

Pivoting the original pattern piece to meet adjustment marks is a simple and accurate method of altering patterns. Once you've adjusted classic styles, you can apply the adjustments to any patterns from that company with no further measuring.

ery pattern book; look for "Fashion Basics" and "Busy Woman's Sewing Patterns" from McCall's; "Basic Very Easy Vogue"; "Jiffy" from Simplicity; "In-Ann-Instant" from Stretch & Sew; and "Burda Super-Easy." Don't bother with the basic-fitting shell patterns. You'll get just as usable results from a classic-style pattern, and you'll be able to wear it when you're done.

Determining your size

Most women buy patterns too large for their body frame, because they use their bust or high-bust measurement. These patterns often don't fit through the neck, shoulders, and front chest area, which are much harder areas to alter than the bust.

Front width	12	12½	13	13½	14	14½	15	15½	16	16½	17	17½
Misses' size	6	8	10	12	14	16	18	20	22			
Junior size	5	7	9	11	13	15						
Half-size		10½	12½	14½	16½	18½	20½	22½	24½			
Women's size							38	40	42	44	46	48

Front Width Fitting Chart

To match the size of your frame to standard pattern sizes, have a friend take your *front width measurement.*

To take this measurement, wear a slip so your friend can find the creases in your skin where your arms meet your body. Measure above the end of the crease, as shown in the drawing at right, across your chest to the other crease, and then round off to the nearest half inch.

You won't find the front width measurement on the back of the pattern envelope, but it's easy to convert that single measurement into your pattern size. The chart on the facing page shows the relationship between the front width and the standard categories of pattern. Don't be surprised if you wind up buying a much smaller pattern; the majority of women are actually sizes 6, 8, and 10.

Once you've selected a pattern, compare your bust, waist, and hip measurements to those on the back of the pattern envelope. Record the difference as a plus (+) or minus (−) measurement.

Changing width by pivoting

Suppose your bust measurement is 37 in. and the measurement on the back of the envelope for your size is 34 in. You need to increase the bustline 3 in. Divide that number by 4, the total number of cut edges at the two side seams. That means you'll now pivot to increase each side seam ¾ in.

Cut out a piece of wax paper, tissue paper, or a non-woven fabric as long as your front pattern piece. This is your worksheet. Don't worry if it isn't wide enough for your pattern. It doesn't have to reach all the way to the center front; it only needs to extend beyond the side seam as much as you need

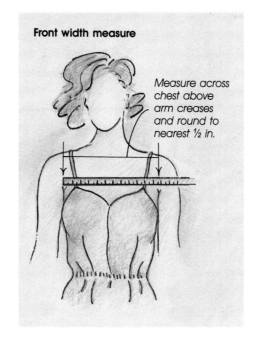

Front width measure

Measure across chest above arm creases and round to nearest ½ in.

for the alteration, as you can see in the drawing below.

If you're using wax paper as a worksheet, place it on a lightly padded work surface (use lightweight wool yardage, thin flannel, or something similar). Then you can easily make all marks with a tracing wheel. The wheel will perforate the wax paper, leaving a connect-the-dots pattern. Otherwise, use your red and black permanent markers to transfer the marks.

Trim all of the pattern pieces to the cutting lines. Place the front pattern piece on top of the worksheet. With a tracing wheel or a black permanent marker, outline the pattern cutting lines on the worksheet. At the underarm, measure ¾ in. out

from the cutting line area and place a mark on the worksheet, as shown in steps 1 and 2 below.

To pivot the pattern for this alteration, place a pin upright at the shoulder where the stitching lines cross. This is a pivot point, which allows the pattern to swing out to meet the alteration mark. Pivot points are always on *seamlines*, while marked changes are always measured from *cutting* lines. Pivot the pattern away from the center front so the cutting line meets the increase mark. With the wheel or the red pen, outline the new armhole cutting line of the pivoted pattern on the worksheet, as shown in steps 3 and 4 below.

Keeping the pattern pivoted, move the pivot pin to the underarm where the stitching lines cross. Pivot the pattern back towards the center so the waist cutting line meets the original outlined waistline, and trace the new side cutting line along the pattern between the underarm and the waistline on the worksheet (step 5).

Tape the pattern to the worksheet, matching the original outline to the old pattern cutting lines (step 6), and cut out the pattern, following the new outline. Apply the same steps to the side seams of the back pattern piece, and you're done.

Notice that you have increased the bust width, but the armhole is the same size as the original pattern. The sleeve will fit smoothly into the armscye.

To increase the waistline or hipline, use the same pivoting principle. For the waistline, simply pivot from the underarm to your new measured waistline adjustment marking, after adjusting the bustline. For the hipline, pivot from the waistline. On a

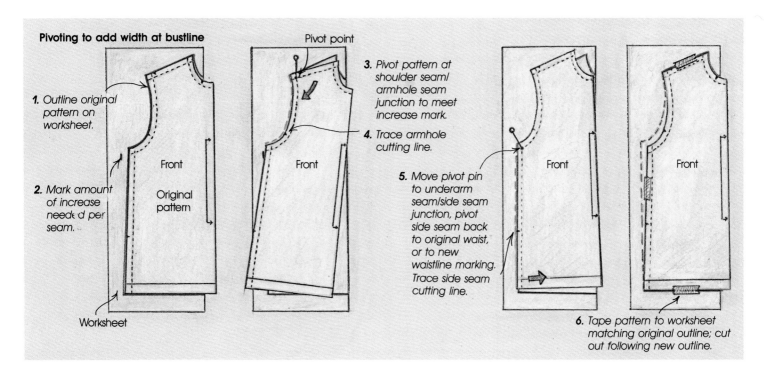

Pivoting to add width at bustline

1. Outline original pattern on worksheet.

2. Mark amount of increase needed per seam.

Front
Original pattern

Worksheet

Pivot point

3. Pivot pattern at shoulder seam/ armhole seam junction to meet increase mark.

4. Trace armhole cutting line.

5. Move pivot pin to underarm seam/side seam junction, pivot side seam back to original waist, or to new waistline marking. Trace side seam cutting line.

Front

Front

Front

6. Tape pattern to worksheet matching original outline; cut out following new outline.

straight skirt, continue any hipline increase evenly to the seam from the hipline to the hemline, to keep the design of the skirt in proportion.

Decreasing at these points simply means to mark the decrease amount inside the traced pattern outline, and pivot from the same points towards the marks. The new cutting line will be inside the original pattern, so after the alterations are made, you may want to fold the original pattern out of the way so you don't cut it when you're cutting the new outline from the worksheet.

Using extensions

The main limitation of pivot-and-slide is that the bustline pivot cannot exceed 1 in. per side seam, for a total increase of 4 in. for the bustline. (Hipline and waist can be increased by any amount.) Pivoting more than 1 in. per side seam at the bustline makes the armhole too high. For increases greater than 4 in., you can use extra extensions, sections added at the underarm of the bodice pattern to give the needed increase beyond pivoting. These sections are added in combination with pivoting techniques and are made by sliding the unpivoted pattern sideways.

Suppose you need 5 in. added to the bust. You can pivot up to 1 in. per side seam, which gives you 4 in. of the needed 5 in. For the remaining inch you'll need to slide the pattern ¼ in. per side seam for the extra extensions. Pivot 1 in., using the technique explained above, then measure out ¼ in. from the new outline at the underarm. Slide the pattern sideways from its original position so the cutting line meets the increase mark and extend the armhole line. Taper the extension to the cutting line at the waistline, as shown in the top drawing at right. Repeat on the back pattern piece. If you add extra extensions to the garment body, you *must* add the same amount (by extension, not by pivoting) to the sleeve, or the sleeve will be too small for the armscye.

Use extra extensions only in combination with pivoting. Without pivoting, an extension does not give the room needed to raise your arm, so the garment would be extremely constricting.

Altering sleeve width

Pivoting to adjust sleeve width is just as simple as the method described above, but you need to compare your own measurement (taken around the fullest part of your upper arm) to the pattern piece, because you won't find the sleeve width on the pattern enve-

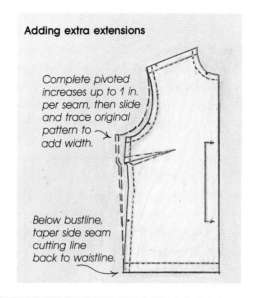

Adding extra extensions

Complete pivoted increases up to 1 in. per seam, then slide and trace original pattern to add width.

Below bustline, taper side seam cutting line back to waistline.

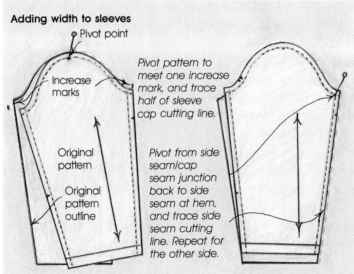

Adding width to sleeves

Pivot point

Increase marks

Original pattern

Original pattern outline

Pivot pattern to meet one increase mark, and trace half of sleeve cap cutting line.

Pivot from side seam/cap seam junction back to side seam at hem, and trace side seam cutting line. Repeat for the other side.

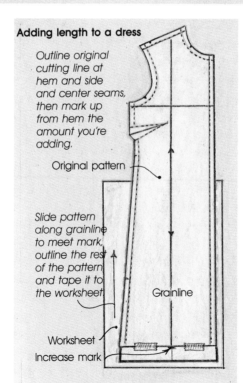

Adding length to a dress

Outline original cutting line at hem and side and center seams, then mark up from hem the amount you're adding.

Original pattern

Slide pattern along grainline to meet mark, outline the rest of the pattern and tape it to the worksheet.

Grainline

Worksheet

Increase mark

lope. Make sure you're working with a pattern that has a basic set-in sleeve, then measure your arm to the nearest half inch, add 2 in. for the minimum basic ease for a standard set-in sleeve, and compare this to the sleeve pattern. Suppose you need to add 1 in. Divide the change by 2 (the number of seams involved), which equals ½ in., then position the pattern on a worksheet and outline the original in marker or with the tracing wheel. At the side seam cutting line just below the cap seam, mark ½ in. away from both sides of the pattern. Place a pin at the dot at the center of the sleeve cap, as shown in the middle drawing at left, and pivot from that point so that the cutting line meets the first increase mark. Trace the new cap seam cutting line, then, keeping the pattern pivoted, move the pivot point to the underarm where the side and cap seams meet. Now pivot the side seam cutting line back to meet the original at the hem and trace the new side seam cutting line. Repeat for the other side, tape the pattern back in its original position, and cut out on the new lines.

Pivoted changes to sleeve width are limited just like bustline changes. If you need to add more than 1 in. per side (2 in. total change) to your sleeves, pivot the first inch, then add the rest by sliding out an extension, as described above.

Pivoting to change shoulder slope

Suppose you need to drop your shoulder line ½ in. to correct for a sloping shoulder. Here's how to pivot the changes. Position the pattern on a worksheet and outline it as before, then make a mark ½ in. down from the cutting line at the shoulder point. Pivot from the point where neckline and shoulder seams cross so that the shoulder cutting line meets the mark; outline the new cutting line. Keeping the pattern pivoted, place a pivot pin at the shoulder seam and armhole seam junction. Then pivot the pattern until the cutting line at the side seam meets the original side seam cutting line, and trace the new armhole cutting line. Repeat for the back.

Changing length by sliding

Sliding pattern pieces keeps the grainline undisturbed and evenly adds or subtracts length without distorting the cutting lines at the side seams. I'll describe here how to lengthen a one-piece dress pattern, but the same principles apply to sleeves, bodices, jackets, and so on.

Cut a worksheet at least as long as the distance from the waist to the bottom cutting line. Draw a long grainline in the middle of the worksheet. Place the front pattern piece on top of the worksheet, matching the grainlines, and outline only the bottom cutting line and 1 in. along the side seam and center front on the worksheet, as shown at the bottom of p. 22.

To lengthen the pattern, measure *up* on the worksheet from the bottom cutting line the needed amount and make a mark. Place the pattern on the original bottom cutting line. Slide the pattern up, following the grainline, until the pattern meets the lengthening mark, then outline the rest of the side seam and center front, blending from the original hemline to the new side seam. Without moving the pattern, tape it to the worksheet. Cut out the pattern, following the new cutting lines. Apply the same steps to the back pattern piece.

To shorten the pattern, simply mark the measured change below the original hemline, and slide the pattern down before tracing around it.

Combining changes

If you make each of several pattern changes you need, one at a time on separate worksheets, you can make them in any order, but as you become more comfortable with the process, you'll want to combine alterations, like changing shoulder slope and bust width at the same time. To combine alterations, make sure you make the changes in this order: Start with any changes to hem length, then adjust centers (back and front) if necessary; then adjust the neckline, then shoulders, then the armhole, the bustline, the waistline, and the hipline.

Here's how to make shoulder and width changes at the same time. Outline the original, as usual, then mark the worksheet for both changes. Pivot the pattern to meet the shoulder mark, and outline the new cutting line. Move the pivot point to the shoulder/armhole seamline crossing, then pivot out to the new bustline measure, and outline the armhole cutting line. Move the pivot point to the underarm, and pivot so the side seam meets the original hemline. Trace, cut, and repeat for the pattern back. □

Nancy Zieman specializes in time-saving techniques for the busy woman. She is the author of The Busy Woman's Fitting Book *($12 postpaid from Nancy's Notions, PO Box 683, Beaver Dam, WI 53916). She also designs "Busy Woman's Sewing Patterns" for the McCall Pattern Company and is the hostess of a public television show,* Sewing With Nancy. *Co-author Robbie Fanning is a contributing editor of* Threads.

Fine-tuning with pivot and slide

I also use pivot-and-slide techniques to fit the garment itself. Ask a friend to help you reach areas that would be difficult for you to reach alone. I machine baste the darts, shoulder seams, center front and back, and side seams (except the zipper opening), sleeve underarm seam, armhole seam for set-in sleeves, and waistline seam. Then I try on the garment, pinning in shoulder pads if the pattern calls for them, and pinning the opening.

I match the garment's center front and back to my figure, pinning to my undergarments. On skirts, I sew a length of 1 in. elastic to fit my waistline and put it on, then pin the skirt to the elastic, matching the waistline stitching line to the horizontal center of the elastic.

Now I check for extra folds of fabric or pull wrinkles, looking at their direction. The chart below provides a visual explanation of what different types of wrinkles signify. Once I understand why the garment is wrinkling, I unbaste, place the altered pattern on the garment piece, and use pivot or slide techniques to adjust the garment.

A common problem that can be solved this way is the horizontal fold wrinkle that occurs on skirts and pants directly below the back waistline, telling you that you have too much length in the center back seam. Pinch out the fold of extra fabric and place a pin at the base of it. Measure the depth of the wrinkle at the deepest part, and double the measurement to determine the extent of the wrinkle.

Take off the garment and remove the dart bastings. On the garment, measure the amount of the wrinkle down from the cutting edge at the center back. Place a marking pin in the fabric at this point. Fold the skirt back or pants in half, right sides together. Place the altered back pattern on top of the actual garment back. Slide the pattern down until the cutting line and marking pin meet. At the center-back stitching line of the pattern, place a pivot pin, and pivot the pattern so its *waistline* stitching line meets the *actual* stitching line of the skirt, as in the drawing below. Trim off the excess fabric, following the pattern cutting line. Save this fabric piece and use it to make the same recutting adjustment on the pattern piece. —N.Z.

Pivoting to fine-tune the fit

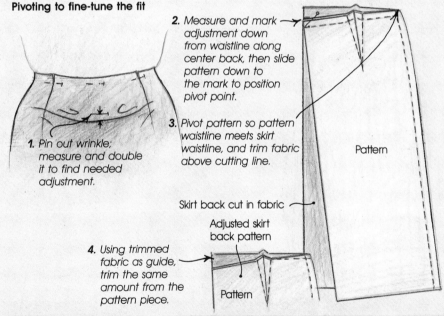

2. Measure and mark adjustment down from waistline along center back, then slide pattern down to the mark to position pivot point.

1. Pin out wrinkle; measure and double it to find needed adjustment.

3. Pivot pattern so pattern waistline meets skirt waistline, and trim fabric above cutting line.

Pattern

Skirt back cut in fabric

Adjusted skirt back pattern

4. Using trimmed fabric as guide, trim the same amount from the pattern piece.

Pattern

WRINKLE CHART		
	Fold wrinkles: Too much fabric	**Pull wrinkles:** Too little fabric
Horizontal	Horizontal fold wrinkles = too much length	Horizontal pull wrinkles = not enough length
Vertical	Vertical fold wrinkles = too much width	Vertical pull wrinkles = not enough width
Bias	Bias fold wrinkles = too much length and width	Bias pull wrinkles = not enough length and not enough width

Off-the-Chart Sizes

Whether you're size 2 or 22, you can grade that pattern to fit

by Nancy Bryant

have you ever wanted to change the size of a sewing pattern because your size is off the charts or because you've borrowed a pattern from a larger or smaller friend? Changing the size of a pattern, called *pattern grading,* isn't hard. If you've ever sewn with a multisize pattern, you probably know more about grading than you may realize.

This article will explain the basics of pattern grading on commercial patterns for a skirt, blouse, and set-in sleeve. The method I've developed is similar to the slash-and-spread method of pattern alteration, and it combines elements of the grading methods used by the garment industry and the commercial pattern industry. Pattern fitting alterations are a separate operation from pattern grading; if you usually make fitting alterations to commercial patterns, you'll need to make the same alterations after you have graded a pattern.

Sizing

The pattern companies have determined the amounts each size is to vary from the next. The sizing measurement charts in pattern catalogs and on pattern instruction sheets indicate these amounts. The measurements we will use for our size standards are shown in the chart at right.

The increment that the bust, waist, and hip circumferences shrink or grow from one size to the next is called the *grade.* An increase of 1 in. (from a size 8 to a size 10) is a 1-in. grade. Logically, if the body measurement in a given area increases by 1 in., the garment circumference and hence the pattern width in that area must also increase by 1 in. The increase is spread around the body in grading increments. As the sizes get larger, the grading increments also get larger, as detailed in the charts on pp. 25, 26, 28, and 29.

The grading procedure is planned to keep the graded pattern centered on the body in the same way the original was. For example, to keep darts centered on the body, the pattern changes in width more toward the side seam than toward the center front, in accordance with the way bodies change shape from one size to the next.

Changes in body measurements and pattern sizes in places other than the bust, waist, and hip differ. For example, the neck circumference changes less than the bust for each pattern size change.

To grade a pattern, you divide it into sections delineated by vertical and horizontal slash lines and cut apart the sections. To *upgrade,* or enlarge, a pattern, you spread the sections by amounts specified in a grading chart, such as the one on p. 26; to *downgrade* a pattern, or make it a smaller size, you overlap the sections. After taping the sections in place, you true the cutting and stitching lines of the pattern where they have been spread or overlapped, using the original pattern as a template wherever possible. If you are larger or smaller than the sizes given in the charts, use the grade increments of the nearest size.

Tools and supplies

You'll need a mechanical pencil or a sharp No. 2 pencil, a good eraser, scissors, and transparent tape as well as your pattern pieces. Keep the original pattern intact; trace it onto tissue or tracing paper. Include notches and all construction symbols. It's better to grade without seam allowances on the pattern. Use a roll or large sheets of graph paper with a ⅛-in. grid, available in art supply stores, as a base on which to lay out the pattern sections. You can use ¼-in.-grid graph paper, but maintaining accuracy will be more difficult. An 18-in. clear plastic ruler with ⅛-in. grid lines in red is helpful. Several colored pencils (red, green, and blue) and a few pattern weights are also useful.

Skirt grading

To clarify the process, we'll first upgrade a basic skirt. A skirt has four grade lines, two for width and two for length. They're defined in the drawing on p. 26.

Basic skirt upgrade—Make a tracing-paper copy of your basic skirt front or skirt front sloper. Lay the traced pattern piece over the graph paper, aligning the center front (CF) of the pattern with a vertical grid line on the graph paper. Draw the vertical and horizontal slash lines on the traced pattern with a red pencil, as shown in the drawing on p. 26. Align each slash line with a graph paper grid line; this will speed the grading process later on. Number the sections from 1 through 9, as shown.

I will upgrade a size 18 skirt pattern to a size 20. If you wish to grade more than one size at a time, simply add together the grading increments for the appropriate sizes. For example, to grade a size 14 skirt to a size 18, spread line A by ⅛ in. plus ³⁄₁₆ in., or ⁵⁄₁₆ in. If you want to downgrade your pattern, overlap the sections.

Slash the pattern on line A and line C to separate section 1 completely from the remainder of the skirt front pattern. Position section 1 on the graph paper so that the CF (center front) line and line C of the pattern align with grid lines of the graph paper, leaving enough space on the graph paper for spreading the rest of the sections. Tape section 1 in place. Next, cut apart section 2 on lines B and C and position it next to section 1, separated by the grade increment given in the grading chart for line A (³⁄₁₆ in. for size 18 to size 20). Keep line C on the same horizontal grid line—it helps to draw a red line on the graph paper grid line that aligns with line C on the pattern pieces. Tape section 2 in place. Continue in sequence, spreading each piece horizontally or vertically by the amount specified in the grading chart. If your height is the same as the standard height for the size you're grading from (according to the chart at the back of the pattern catalog), you can omit the length adjustments (lines C and D) from the pattern grade. ⇨

From *Threads* magazine (June 1990) 29:58-63

STANDARD BODY MEASUREMENTS (IN INCHES)

	1-in. grade between sizes 4, 6, 8, and 10				1½-in. grade between sizes 10, 12, 14, and 16			2-in. grade between sizes 16, 18, 20, and 22		
Size	4	6	8	10	12	14	16	18	20	22
Bust	29½	30½	31½	32½	34	35½	37	39	41	43
Waist	22	23	24	25	26½	28	29½	31½	33½	35½
Hip	31½	32½	33½	34½	36	37½	39	41	43	45

For sewers who can't buy patterns that fit, Nancy Bryant's grading system is the answer. Once you learn how to spread or overlap a pattern along five lines on the bodice and four on the skirt, the world of commercial patterns is open to you. Shown here, Folkwear's Sporty Forties pattern is graded down to a size 4 and up to a size 18 (Photo by Susan Kahn)

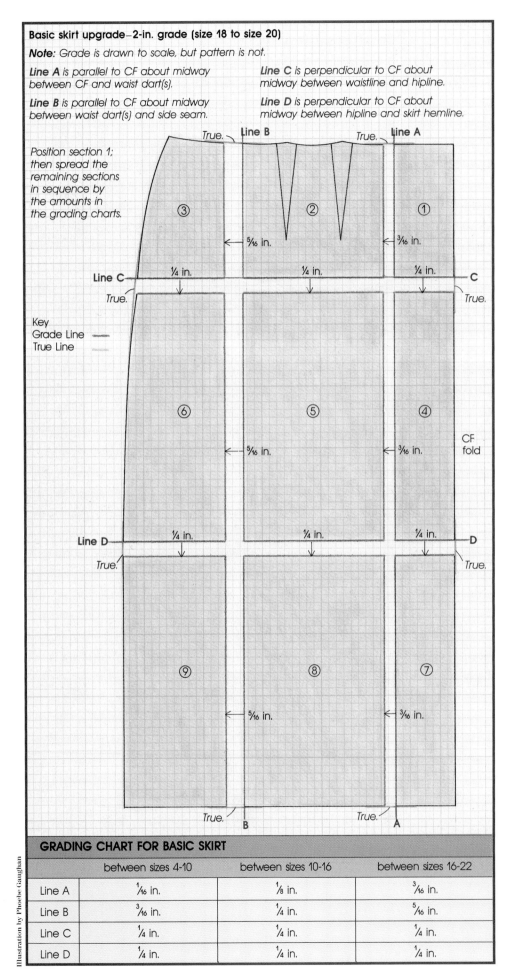

Basic skirt upgrade—2-in. grade (size 18 to size 20)

Note: Grade is drawn to scale, but pattern is not.

Line A *is parallel to CF about midway between CF and waist dart(s).*

Line B *is parallel to CF about midway between waist dart(s) and side seam.*

Line C *is perpendicular to CF about midway between waistline and hipline.*

Line D *is perpendicular to CF about midway between hipline and skirt hemline.*

Position section 1; then spread the remaining sections in sequence by the amounts in the grading charts.

Key
Grade Line ——
True Line ——

Line B   True.   Line A   True.

③   ②   ①

5/16 in.   3/16 in.

Line C   1/4 in.   1/4 in.   1/4 in.   C
True.   True.

⑥   ⑤   ④

5/16 in.   3/16 in.   CF fold

Line D   1/4 in.   1/4 in.   1/4 in.   D
True.   True.

⑨   ⑧   ⑦

5/16 in.   3/16 in.

True.   B   True.   A

GRADING CHART FOR BASIC SKIRT

	between sizes 4-10	between sizes 10-16	between sizes 16-22
Line A	1/16 in.	1/8 in.	3/16 in.
Line B	3/16 in.	1/4 in.	5/16 in.
Line C	1/4 in.	1/4 in.	1/4 in.
Line D	1/4 in.	1/4 in.	1/4 in.

Trueing—After taping down all the sections, you must true the seamlines or cutting lines where there are gaps as a result of the spreading (or overlapping, in the case of a downgrade). I use a green pencil to indicate the final trued lines. For straight lines, such as the center front, use a ruler to connect the endpoints of the seamlines and cutting lines of the new graded pattern. For curved lines, such as the hipline, you can use the original pattern as a template to trace the shape of the new pattern edges, or you can use a hip curve ruler.

Before trueing an edge with a dart, such as the waistline, first fold the dart closed in the direction it would be pressed. Then use the original skirt pattern, with its waist dart pinned or taped closed, as a template. Center the original skirt pattern beneath the new graded pattern and trace the curved shape of the waistline.

Grade the skirt back in the same way, positioning the slash lines where you positioned them for the front. Check that all seamlines that will be sewn together are the same length and that notches match.

Now that you've completed the skirt grade you can see how the grading increments directly relate to body measurements. The changes at lines A and B, which affect the waist and the hip measurements, have added 8/16 in. (3/16 in. at line A and 5/16 in. at line B) in width to half the skirt front, or 1 in. to the whole skirt front. After the same changes have been made to the back, the increase to the waist and hip measurements would be 2 in., which is just what we'd expect for a 2-in. grade. Adding up the grading increments and checking them against the grading chart is a good way to check your work.

Grading a stylized skirt pattern—Now we'll look at the grading process for a stylized skirt design with multiple pieces, such as the flared skirt with yoke and waistband shown in the drawing at right. First lay out and study the pattern pieces so you understand how they fit together and what each notch represents. Sketching the pattern pieces and their slash lines helps me to think through the grade, see how the pieces relate, and anticipate problems.

When seamlines cross grading sections, the grade increments must be applied to both parts. For example, the seamline between the yoke and the lower skirt crosses sections 4, 5, and 6, so we have to create these sections on both pattern pieces. Draw line B between the notch and CF on both the yoke and the lower skirt patterns so that the notches will match after grading. Slash and spread in sequence the sections of each pattern piece by the amounts specified in the grading chart, as for the basic skirt. Grade the skirt back the same, positioning the slash lines where you did for the front.

In order for the construction markings on the waistband to match those on the skirt, the waistband must increase proportionately at left front, right front, left back, and right back. To grade the waistband pattern, draw slash lines between CF and side seams on both left and right sides and between side seams and CB (center back) on both left and right sides. Add the width increases made to the skirt at lines A and B to arrive at the increase needed at each of these four slashes. In this example $\frac{3}{16}$ in. plus $\frac{5}{16}$ in. equals $\frac{8}{16}$ in.—the waistband must be spread $\frac{1}{2}$ in. at each slash line.

Bodice grading

The bodice is more complex to grade than the skirt because the width and length changes on the bodice do not remain constant along the slash lines. The changes are smaller above the chest than they are below. For example, according to the bodice grading chart on p. 28, when a pattern is upgraded from a size 18 to a size 20, line A is spread $\frac{1}{16}$ in. above line D and $\frac{3}{16}$ in. below it. There are two adjustment lines for width and three for length. They are defined in the drawing on p. 28.

Grading a basic bodice—To practice grading a bodice front, we'll do a 2-in. upgrade, from size 18 to size 20. Trace your pattern. Draw the red slash lines, aligning them with grid lines, as shown in the drawing.

Number the bodice sections 1 through 11 as shown. Again, position the pattern over the graph paper so that CF aligns with a vertical grid line. Spread the sections in sequence according to the amounts in the chart.

When you grade the back bodice, put the slash lines in locations similar to those on the front bodice. For example, if you've put line E slightly above the side seam notch on the blouse front, put it the same distance from the notch on the blouse back.

The armscye is the most difficult curve to true. I begin at line D near the armscye notch by marking the midpoint of the jog in the original seamline with a short line. Then I use the armscye curve of the original pattern as a template to true a new curve from the mark up to line C and then down to the underarm.

The armscye notch must remain the same distance from the underarm seam that it was in the original pattern. Either walk the original pattern along the new armscye seamline to mark the distance, or measure the distance on the original pattern from the underarm seam to the notch with a tape measure and mark the graded

pattern accordingly. The remainder of the armscye curve above line C is a gentle, easy-to-true curve.

With a ruler redraw the waist-fitting dart from the original dart point to the original dart ends. With the bust-fitting dart folded closed in the direction it will be pressed, true the side seamline in a straight line between the two endpoints and trace the shape of the dart end. Fold the waist-fitting dart closed to true the gentle waistline curve.

Draw the shoulder line as a straight line between neckline and armscye. On the back bodice, first fold the shoulder-fitting dart closed. Check that all seamlines that will be sewn together are the same length and that notches match.

Grading a stylized blouse pattern—A stylized blouse pattern is often more complex

to grade than a stylized skirt, partly because of the bodice's additional grading sections, but also because blouses often have more detailing–tucks or pleats for example–and more pattern pieces, such as collars and cuffs. Some styles might be too complicated to tackle. The bodice and sleeve grading charts in this article do not work for blouses with deep armscyes or for raglan or kimono sleeves.

The blouse design shown on p. 29 is moderately complex. The absence of bust-fitting darts, waist darts, or back shoulder darts simplifies the grade, but the front pleats, button band, collar, and cuffs require thought and planning.

After thinking through the grading decisions, such as whether you want to increase the width of the front band or the cuff, trace all the pattern pieces (including seam

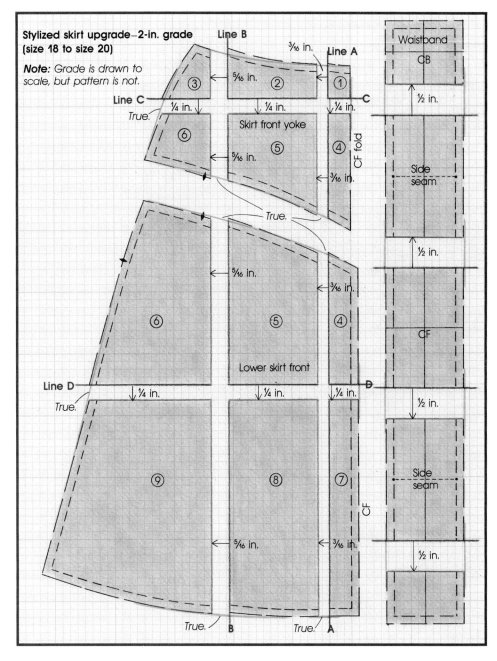

Stylized skirt upgrade–2-in. grade (size 18 to size 20)

Note: Grade is drawn to scale, but pattern is not.

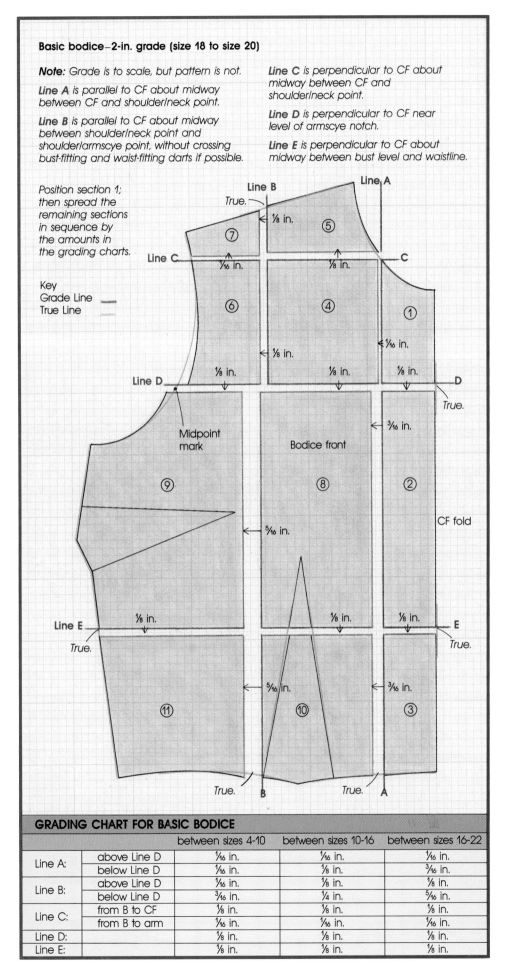

Basic bodice–2-in. grade (size 18 to size 20)

Note: Grade is to scale, but pattern is not.

Line A is parallel to CF about midway between CF and shoulder/neck point.

Line B is parallel to CF about midway between shoulder/neck point and shoulder/armscye point, without crossing bust-fitting and waist-fitting darts if possible.

Line C is perpendicular to CF about midway between CF and shoulder/neck point.

Line D is perpendicular to CF near level of armscye notch.

Line E is perpendicular to CF about midway between bust level and waistline.

Position section 1; then spread the remaining sections in sequence by the amounts in the grading charts.

GRADING CHART FOR BASIC BODICE		between sizes 4-10	between sizes 10-16	between sizes 16-22
Line A:	above Line D	1/16 in.	1/16 in.	1/16 in.
	below Line D	1/16 in.	1/8 in.	3/16 in.
Line B:	above Line D	1/16 in.	1/8 in.	1/8 in.
	below Line D	3/16 in.	1/4 in.	5/16 in.
Line C:	from B to CF	1/8 in.	1/8 in.	1/8 in.
	from B to arm	1/16 in.	1/16 in.	1/16 in.
Line D:		1/8 in.	1/8 in.	1/8 in.
Line E:		1/8 in.	1/8 in.	1/8 in.

allowances) on tracing paper, and mark notches, grainlines, and construction symbols. Draw the red slash lines on the traced copies. Whenever possible, plan the slash lines to avoid pleats, plackets, and other design details. Orient the pattern pieces on the graph paper in the same way they will be on the body. The easiest way to do this is to align the seamlines that will be sewn together. For example, after I'd graded the bodice front, I positioned the front yoke pattern piece so that its lower edge was parallel to the shoulder seamline of the bodice front.

This blouse, like the stylized skirt, has seamlines that cross grading sections: The front band seamline crosses sections 1, 2, and 3, and the front yoke seamline crosses sections 4 and 7. Thus, we have to create these sections on the blouse front pattern as well as on the front yoke pattern and the front band pattern. Furthermore, because the front yoke pattern is so small, we must break line C into two sections so that it intersects both the neck curve and the armscye curve. Draw line B between the notch and the side seam on both the front yoke and blouse front patterns, so that the notches will match after grading. As shown in the drawing at right, position the grading sections according to the numbered sequence, using the grading increments in the basic bodice grading chart.

Sleeves–This stylized sleeve is different from a basic sleeve in that the lower portion of the sleeve is pleated into a cuff and there is no elbow dart. I chose not to change the width of the cuff, so I've eliminated the slash line that would affect this change and applied the sleeve length grade entirely to the sleeve pattern piece. If I had chosen to widen the cuff, I would have applied one quarter of the total sleeve length grade to the cuff and the remaining three quarters of the sleeve length grade to the sleeve. The cuff length increases match the increases made to the width of the lower portion of the sleeve at lines A and B.

After grading the sleeve, re-mark the sleeve armscye notch by walking the original sleeve pattern along the new armscye seamline. This will ensure that the armscye notches on the graded blouse and sleeve patterns match. Make sure the sleeve cap has the same amount of ease as the original sleeve cap. If it does not, adjust the sleeve cap sections.

I chose not to change the width of the front band, and so I applied only the length grades (at lines D and E) to the band and the complete width grade to the blouse front. Thus, at lines A and B the bodice width increased by the same amounts as for the basic bodice. I respaced the buttonhole markings on the front band after completing the grade.

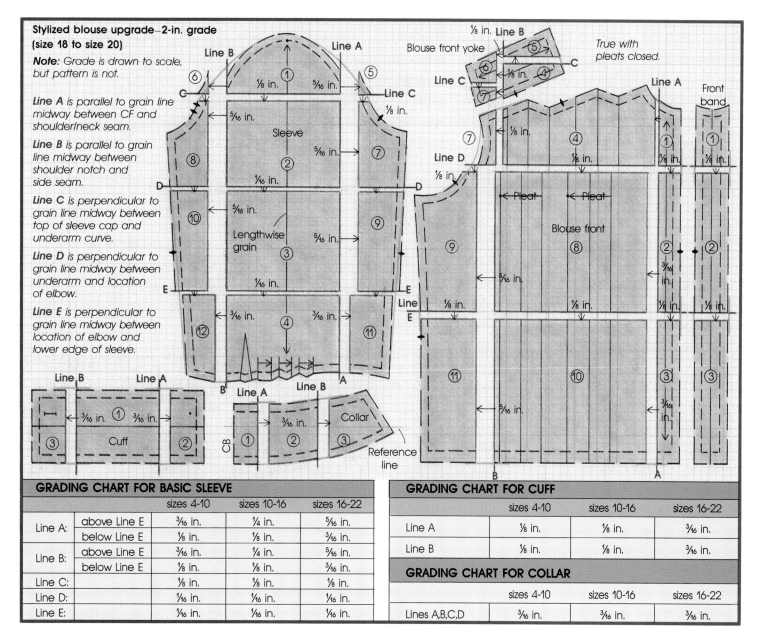

Stylized blouse upgrade—2-in. grade (size 18 to size 20)

Note: Grade is drawn to scale, but pattern is not.

Line A is parallel to grain line midway between CF and shoulder/neck seam.

Line B is parallel to grain line midway between shoulder notch and side seam.

Line C is perpendicular to grain line midway between top of sleeve cap and underarm curve.

Line D is perpendicular to grain line midway between underarm and location of elbow.

Line E is perpendicular to grain line midway between location of elbow and lower edge of sleeve.

Blouse front yoke

True with pleats closed.

Front band

GRADING CHART FOR BASIC SLEEVE		sizes 4-10	sizes 10-16	sizes 16-22
Line A:	above Line E	³⁄₁₆ in.	¼ in.	⁵⁄₁₆ in.
	below Line E	⅛ in.	⅛ in.	³⁄₁₆ in.
Line B:	above Line E	³⁄₁₆ in.	¼ in.	⁵⁄₁₆ in.
	below Line E	⅛ in.	⅛ in.	³⁄₁₆ in.
Line C:		⅛ in.	⅛ in.	⅛ in.
Line D:		¹⁄₁₆ in.	¹⁄₁₆ in.	¹⁄₁₆ in.
Line E:		¹⁄₁₆ in.	¹⁄₁₆ in.	¹⁄₁₆ in.

GRADING CHART FOR CUFF	sizes 4-10	sizes 10-16	sizes 16-22
Line A	⅛ in.	⅛ in.	³⁄₁₆ in.
Line B	⅛ in.	⅛ in.	³⁄₁₆ in.

GRADING CHART FOR COLLAR	sizes 4-10	sizes 10-16	sizes 16-22
Lines A,B,C,D	³⁄₁₆ in.	³⁄₁₆ in.	³⁄₁₆ in.

Collar—I decided not to change the collar width. However, the collar must be graded so that its neck edge length will fit the neckline of the graded blouse, so a grading chart and slash lines are required.

Because this collar pattern is of half the collar, we'll apply half the total neck edge increase in two places. (If the collar pattern were of the whole collar, we'd apply the total neck edge increase at four slash lines.) We divide the half-collar with two slash lines, as shown in the drawing above, so that construction symbols match those of the blouse neckline. The blue line perpendicular to the center back is a reference line that aids in keeping the collar sections aligned.

Depending on the degree of curve in the collar's neck edge, the standard collar grade increments may not yield a collar neck edge the same length as the blouse neckline. Measure the neckline length on

the graded blouse and adjust the collar grade increments accordingly.

Facings, flaps, and pockets—You can usually trace the facings for necklines, armscyes, and front closures from the graded pattern, but some details, such as inset pockets, must be graded separately. To grade underlays, flaps, or pockets that extend from side seam to center front, use the portion of the grading chart that affects those areas.

Often there is no one grading solution; grading problems have different interpretations. One person might grade a patch pocket for each size change, so that the pocket would stay in proportion; another might keep the patch pocket the same size for all sizes; and a third might grade it to a small size for sizes 4 to 10, a medium for sizes 12 to 16, and a large for sizes 18 to 22. Each of these solutions is acceptable. □

Nancy Bryant wrote about modern garments with vintage styles in "Historic Chic," Threads, No. 18, p. 38. She is an assistant professor in the Apparel Design Program at Oregon State University in Corvallis, OR.

Further reading

Price, Jeanne, and Bernard Zamkoff. *Grading Techniques for Modern Design.* New York: Fairchild Publications, 1974. *Focuses on junior and missy bodice, sleeve, and skirt grading from an apparel manufacturer's viewpoint.*

Taylor, Patrick, and Martin Shoben. *Grading for the Fashion Industry, the Theory and Practice.* London: Hutchinson and Co., Ltd. 1984. *A complex and comprehensive text, also from an apparel manufacturer's viewpoint. Includes a survey of 34 body measurements (in metric) as well as two- and three-dimensional grading for missy bodices, skirts, sleeves, and pants.*

Fitting Jacket Shoulders

Trying on ready-to-wear will show you the pattern changes you need

by Mary Roehr

Like many apparently overwhelming projects, even jacket fitting begins to look manageable once you know where to start. And since jackets hang from the shoulders, it makes sense to start fitting them there. In fact, tailors consider well-fit shoulders to be the key to a well-fitted jacket.

But even if you tackle the shoulders first, there's a more logical place to begin any fitting project, and that's by taking a good look at yourself in ready-to-wear clothes, either those you own or by trying on clothes in stores. By observing the way you fit in typical ready-to-wear, you'll get a good preview of what unaltered sewing patterns will look like on you.

For each of the four most common shoulder fitting issues I'll discuss on the following pages (shoulder width, shoulder slope, uneven shoulders, and rounded upper back), let's begin with a look at how the problem will present itself in a finished jacket. Then we'll examine how to measure the area in question, and see how to alter the pattern accordingly. Some people will also have to consider the fitting issues at bust and sleeves, but since jackets aren't close-fitting garments in these areas, many figures can be fit to perfection in them with only shoulder corrections plus minor length and circumference adjustments at the hems and side seams.

As with any major sewing project, you'll certainly want to make a muslin test version of your jacket pattern, but all the adjustments described here should be done to the pattern before cutting the muslin. Of course, you'll find it easier to take the measurements and evaluate the fit of ready-to-wear garments if you're working with a friend. Let's start with the issue of width.

Shoulder width, or jacket width?

Tailors typically measure shoulder width from armhole seamline to seamline at the shoulder level on a jacket their client is wearing. This is because the seamlines on the jacket give a definite point of reference, unlike the ends of the shoulder bones, which can be hard to locate exactly. I suggest you do the same thing with your favorite jacket. Even if the jacket doesn't fit perfectly, or if you're making a different style, you can see if the seams should be narrower or wider and by how much.

If you don't have a jacket to measure, try placing short strips of tape on your back (or on a snug T-shirt) from just above your underarms to the ends of your shoulders, about where armhole seams would fall on a well-fitting blouse. Measure across the upper back, curving over the most prominent neckbone from

The way you fit in ready-to-wear is a good preview of how you'll look in unaltered sewing patterns

the top of one tape to the other. Your jacket should measure at least ½ in. beyond this measure on each side, or wider, depending on the shoulder pad emphasis you want.

How shoulder pads affect fitting

Since garments aren't as fitted as they used to be, and many shoulder lines are exaggerated, there are no longer definite rules for shoulder width. Shoulders on some oversized jacket patterns extend as much as 3 in. on each side past the normal shoulders. My opinion is that shoulder pads can't adequately support a jacket more than 1½ in. past the normal shoulder without forming creases like those in the photo on the facing page, so I

cut mine back to this width or narrower. When most women complain that they hate shoulder pads, it's usually because their jacket shoulders are too wide. Cutting them back to 1½ in. past the wearer's shoulders usually helps.

Shoulder pads obviously affect shoulder height, described on p. 32, as well as width. Different pad thicknesses can usually conceal deviations in shoulder height of less than ½ in. from what the pattern considers normal (to measure your slope, see the top left drawing on p. 32). To avoid overaltering, which can make your garments look strange even if they fit, I recommend subtracting ½ in. from the total amount your shoulder slope differs from the normal slope. For example, if your shoulder slope is ¾ in. from the norm, only alter the pattern ¼ in. and pad or remove padding to make up the difference.

Redrawing the shoulder seamline

Three of the alterations described here require altering the shoulder seamline, so once you're wearing the muslin test, check to see if the seamline is running straight along the top of your shoulder from neck to arm, without angling to the front or the back, particularly if you've had to alter for a rounded upper back. This is purely a visual consideration; the jacket should fit well whether the seamline angles or not. Shifting it (see *Basics, Threads* No. 49) shouldn't affect the fit, since you merely add back to one side what you remove from the other. It can, however, definitely improve the appearance of the jacket. ⇨

Mary Roehr operated a custom tailoring/ alterations business for 15 years and has written four books on the subject, available from Book Masters at (800) 247-6553.

From *Threads* magazine (October 1993) 49:62-65

Adjusting shoulder width: *When jacket shoulders are too wide (left) (usually because shoulder padding is exaggerated), they droop off the ends of the shoulder, and vertical wrinkles form across the entire back. The pads' shape may also be apparent under the jacket fabric. Too-tight shoulders (right) are as obvious from their discomfort as from their appearance. Measuring for and deciding on appropriate width is described on the facing page. The alteration below allows you to shift the position of the armhole without significantly changing its length, so you won't have to make any corresponding changes to the sleeve cap.*

Back is shown; make same change to front.
No seam allowances are shown.

3. *Cut shoulder section free, and move horizontally the desired amount: out to widen, or in to narrow shoulders.*

1. *Draw a horizontal line halfway through armscye.*

2. *Draw a vertical line halfway through shoulder seam.*

To widen

4. *True shoulder and armscye seamlines (dotted lines).*

To narrow

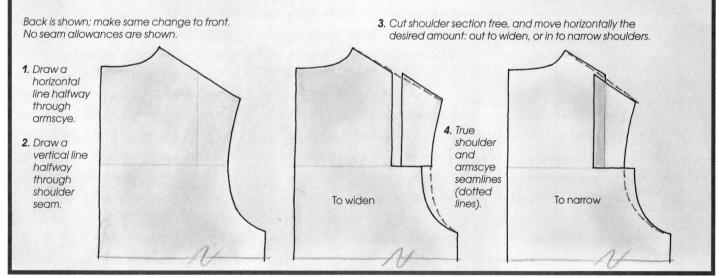

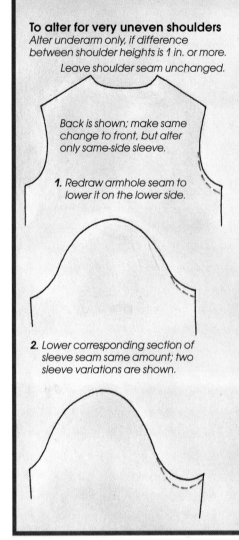

To alter for very uneven shoulders

Alter underarm only, if difference between shoulder heights is 1 in. or more.

Leave shoulder seam unchanged.

Back is shown; make same change to front, but alter only same-side sleeve.

1. *Redraw armhole seam to lower it on the lower side.*

2. *Lower corresponding section of sleeve seam same amount; two sleeve variations are shown.*

Checking and correcting shoulder height: Your shoulder height determines whether your shoulders are sloped, normal, or erect as compared to the pattern. If you have very sloping shoulders, drag lines may radiate up from the bottom of the armhole because your shoulders are not supporting the garment's shoulders, or a single vertical fold may appear right next to the armscye on the jacket body, as you can see on the left-hand shoulder in the photo on the facing page. The photo above shows the typical roll of fabric that appears below the back of the collar on erect shoulders. There may also be tension lines radiating down from the ends of the too-high shoulders.

To measure shoulder height, place a carpenters' level (or a yardstick held level by eye) vertically across the back of the shoulders and on top of the most prominent neckbone. When it's parallel to the floor, measure the distance from the level or yardstick to the end of the shoulders, as shown below. A 2-in. slope is what the pattern companies use, so more than 2 in. is sloping and less than 2 in. is erect. Notice that the alteration for shoulder height moves the whole armhole up or down as needed and so the sleeve is not affected.

Back is shown; make same change to front.

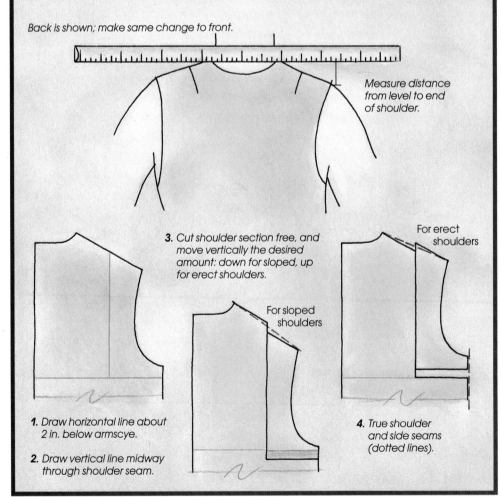

Measure distance from level to end of shoulder.

3. *Cut shoulder section free, and move vertically the desired amount: down for sloped, up for erect shoulders.*

For erect shoulders

For sloped shoulders

1. *Draw horizontal line about 2 in. below armscye.*

2. *Draw vertical line midway through shoulder seam.*

4. *True shoulder and side seams (dotted lines).*

Uneven shoulders: *As you may have noticed when measuring your shoulder height, it's very common for one shoulder to be lower than the other, whether you're sloped, normal, or erect overall. In a jacket, the low shoulder will often have a vertical fold from the bottom of the armscye towards the shoulder, as on the left side of the jacket pictured. Since you don't want to appear uneven, it's better to make the shoulders the same and then pad the lower one to fill in the excess, than to fit each shoulder perfectly. If the difference between the shoulders is great, usually more than 1 in., you also have to lower the armhole for the low shoulder, because it's not just the top of the shoulder that's lower, it's the entire arm socket. In this extreme case, you can still cut and pad the shoulders to appear symmetrical, but the armscyes will be different, so the sleeve also has to be altered, as shown in the drawings on the facing page.*

Rounded upper back: *Also known as kyphosis, or "dowager's hump," a rounded upper back will cause drag lines radiating down and outward from the protrusion, and sometimes also wrinkles across the shoulder seam. To determine the amount of extra length the roundness needs for fit, measure down the person's center back from the most prominent neckbone to the waist. By extending the center back the required distance to match the measurement, as shown in the drawing below, you're also creating a small neckline dart that, together with the reshaped center-back seam, contours the back to the roundness. You will definitely need to make a muslin in this case (especially to fine-tune the shape of the center-back seam), but the extra work is worth it.*

Make changes to back only.

1. Draw line A horizontally through armscye.

2. Draw line B vertically halfway through neckline.

3. Slash line A to, but not through, armscye.

4. Slash line B to, but not through, line A.

5. Spread line A to add measured extra length. This creates a neckline dart at line B, which you sew closed like any other dart.

6. Redraw center-back curve as needed (check on muslin).

Illustrations by Phoebe Gaughan

Narrowing an Extended Shoulder

Combining patterns will give you the silhouette you want

by Margaret Komives

Sleeve profiles

Dropped shoulder

Extended shoulder

Slightly extended shoulder

Semi-fitted shoulder

Dropped shoulder has a very shallow cap. Extended shoulder has a slightly shallow cap. Slightly extended shoulder has a slightly broad and deep shaped cap. Semi-fitted shoulder has a well-shaped cap.

Current fashion in classic shirts and blouses is more often than not an extended, softly padded shoulder. But many sewers would prefer a shoulder with a sleeve seam nearer to the natural shoulder line. A narrower, more squared shoulder tends to give a taller, slimmer look and is often preferred by a short person or one who wears a larger size. In addition, the higher armscye of the more fitted sleeve fits more comfortably under most suit jackets.

To determine the sleeve style before purchasing a pattern, read the description, if there is one, or look at the sketch of the sleeve pattern on the instruction sheet in the pattern envelope. Compare the description or the sketch to the profiles in the drawing above. Don't rely on the fashion drawing on the envelope; it is not always accurate. If a pattern description does not mention the sleeve style, it is probably semi-fitted.

If you already have a pattern you want to use but don't like its extended or dropped shoulder, it's not difficult to alter. Your first inclination might be to reduce the shoulder width by moving the armscye seam toward the neck. But this would require a drastic change to the sleeve. Except for minor alterations, you almost always must use a sleeve pattern with the armscye designed for it. Instead, the solution is to transfer the patterns for an armscye, a shoulder, and a sleeve you do like to the pattern whose sleeve and shoulder you don't like.

First find a pattern in your collection that has both a sleeve and a shoulder that you prefer. Keep in mind that it is the armscye, side seam, and probably part of the shoulder seamline that you will be altering. Try to find a pattern whose shoulder slope and waist-to-shoulder ease are similar to those in your current pattern, because this will make the patterns easier to combine.

From *Threads* magazine (June 1992) 41:46-47

Preparing the patterns

The first step is to simplify the bodices of both your current pattern and the pre-ferred-shoulder pattern to their basic lines. This involves temporarily eliminat-ing any styling details that affect the shoulder and armscye areas, such as a yoke or a shoulder seam that is forward of the actual shoulder line, as shown in step 1 of the drawing at right.

Trace a copy of the pattern elements you must move, using tissue paper or pattern-tracing material and a soft lead pencil, so that you can later restore the patterns to their original lines. Trace both seam and cutting lines. Use removable tape to affix the traced copy to the pattern. When you slash a pattern that includes seam al-lowances, as in the examples in step 1, add a seam allowance to each slashed edge. When joining previously separate sections, align their stitching lines. Note that whenever the shoulder seam of a pat-tern does not fall along the shoulder line, the shoulder line will be marked, often by small circles or a square.

In addition, fold out details such as a back pleat, tucks, gathers, a hidden plack-et sewn in one with the front, and so on, to achieve a basic bodice. If there is a sepa-rate button placket band for the front, make a tracing as described earlier and tape it to the bodice in order to determine the center front.

The result of these temporary correc-tions is that you will have two simplified bodice fronts and two simplified bodice backs, all with shoulder seamline at the proper shoulder line. You will return the design details to their original positions after you have transferred the shoulder, armscye, and underarm seams from one pattern to the other.

Transferring the shoulder lines

Superimpose the bodice front of the pre-ferred-shoulder pattern onto the bodice front of your current pattern, as shown in step 2 of the drawing, aligning their center-front lines, and, as closely as pos-sible, the shoulder seams. Do the same with the back. Taping tissue where need-ed to fill in gaps, trace the shoulder, arm-scye, and underarm from the preferred-shoulder pattern onto your current pattern. Then remove the preferred-shoulder pattern. Release gathers, tucks, plackets, and so forth from your current pattern and restore styling details. Your current pattern now has the preferred shoulder and armscye. Use the sleeve from the preferred-shoulder pattern, with no changes, and follow its shoulder pad recommendations.

Make and keep a copy of the simplified

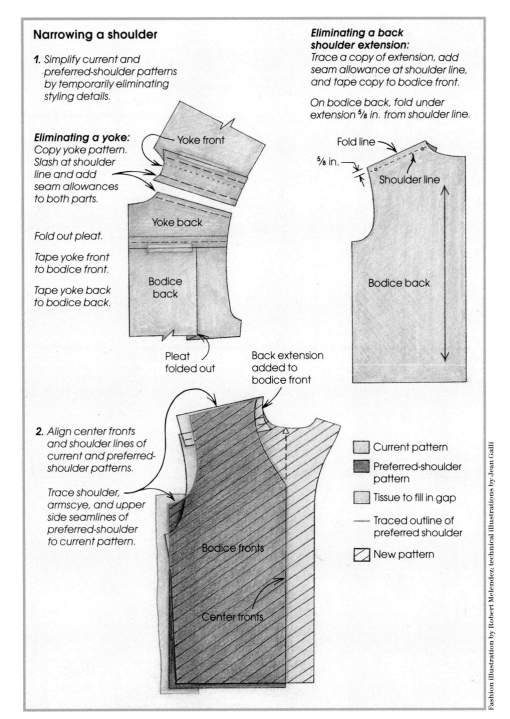

Narrowing a shoulder

1. Simplify current and preferred-shoulder patterns by temporarily eliminating styling details.

Eliminating a yoke:
Copy yoke pattern. Slash at shoulder line and add seam allowances to both parts.

Fold out pleat.

Tape yoke front to bodice front.

Tape yoke back to bodice back.

Yoke front

Yoke back

Bodice back

Pleat folded out

Back extension added to bodice front

Eliminating a back shoulder extension:
Trace a copy of extension, add seam allowance at shoulder line, and tape copy to bodice front.

On bodice back, fold under extension ⅝ in. from shoulder line.

Fold line

⅝ in.

Shoulder line

Bodice back

2. Align center fronts and shoulder lines of current and preferred-shoulder patterns.

Trace shoulder, armscye, and upper side seamlines of preferred-shoulder to current pattern.

Bodice fronts

Center fronts

☐ Current pattern

■ Preferred-shoulder pattern

☐ Tissue to fill in gap

— Traced outline of preferred shoulder

▨ New pattern

version of the preferred-shoulder pat-tern's bodice so that you can use it with other patterns in the future. Keep with it a copy of the sleeve as well.

With the patterns I worked on, the shoulder seams of the current pattern, which had a yoke, fell below those of the preferred-shoulder pattern, because the shoulder line of the former was slightly rounded. To bring the two shoulder seams together, I added the difference to the top of the bodice section, rather than to the yoke. It is not advisable to alter the yoke because it will distort the neckline and center-front line. Naturally it would have been easier if I had used a pattern with-

out a yoke—I could simply have added to the shoulder seam to bring the patterns into alignment.

Since your patterns will likely have dif-ferent degrees of ease—your current pat-tern may be loose fitting and the pattern with the more fitted sleeve may be semi-fitted—you may find it easier to combine, say, the size 10 of the loose-fitting gar-ment with the size 12 of the semi-fitted one, because their widths are almost ex-actly the same. If lengths differ, retain the length of your current pattern. □

Margaret Komives is a frequent contribu-tor to Threads.

Fashion illustration by Robert Melendez; technical illustrations by Jean Galli

Turning Darts into Pleats

Simple pattern alterations transform a plain pattern into a personal design

by Jann Jasper

Varying a darted blouse pattern with pleats

Pleats provide the same shaping as darts, but give a softer look and a little extra ease.

Basic darted blouse pattern can be the foundation for many variations.

Bringing the legs of the darts together but not stitching them creates simple pleats.

Rotating the waist darts of a simple blouse to the shoulder and turning them into pleats created the graceful asymmetrical blouse shown above.

*W*e usually think of the pleat as a way of adding fullness—the classic pleated skirt and the poet sleeve come to mind. But pleats can also be fitting devices, replacing darts. If you examine a commercial pattern and see only pleats, and no darts, it's likely that the shaping, usually accomplished by darts, is in the pleats. The soft fold of a pleat can be preferable when comfort or figure flattery calls for more ease. Sometimes a fabric isn't suited for darts: A dart might form a jarring line in a beautiful print, and darts are difficult to handle in hard-to-sew fabrics, such as metallic or sequined fabric. Pleats can add design interest, and a pleat that's deeper than the dart it replaces provides graceful added fullness. The drawings and photo on the facing page show a couple of examples of pleats derived from darts.

Replacing darts with pleats is a way to vary commercial patterns that you already have in your collection and extend their mileage. You can easily transform bust or shoulder darts in a blouse or jacket or hip darts in a pant or skirt into pleats to create a different look. The blouse in the photo on the facing page was created by rotating the shaping of the waist darts of a simple blouse (also shown) to the shoulder and then turning them into pleats.

I'll use the bust darts in a blouse as an example to show how you can use this patternmaking device. You must start with a darted pattern that fits you properly. Make any fitting adjustments to the pattern before you begin.

If the apex is not marked on your pattern, you need to locate it. Bisect the dart with a straight line that extends about 2 in. past the dart point. Pin the pattern front and back together at the shoulder and side seamlines. Put on the bra you'll wear with the finished garment, and if the pattern calls for shoulder pads, pin them to your bra straps. Then put the pattern on yourself, aligning it at center front, center back, and waist, and pin it to your bra. Mark the pattern at the fullest part of your bust. Since you're working with a pattern that fits you, your apex should be on or close to the line bisecting the dart. My pattern had two waist darts per side, and my apex was between them. Remove the pattern, and draw the legs of the dart to the apex, as shown below. This is the patternmakers' dart for this garment for your body; it encodes the information you need for a proper fit.

Now you're ready to play with darts. A dart (and, by extension, a pleat) can be pivoted to any location around the apex without changing a garment's fit (although it does change the design, of course). The procedure for rotating a dart is explained in *Basics, Threads* No. 46, p. 16. If you're skeptical that you can rotate a dart anywhere, try this: Prepare several bodice drafts, leaving a couple of inches extra paper beyond the seam allowances. On each, rotate the bust dart to a different location. For this experiment, leave the darts as patternmakers' darts.

Then, with their darts pinned and center fronts aligned, stack up your drafts. Voila! The bust shaping of all the drafts is the same!

Pleats

You can replace any dart with a pleat without changing the garment's fit. The most basic way to do this is simply not to stitch the sides of the dart together. Instead, fold the fabric to bring the dart legs together. Then baste along the seamline to hold the pleat in place until you sew the seam. Or, stitch from the edge of the fabric partway along the dart stitching line; the length of stitching will depend on the length of the dart and on the design. Whether or not you partially stitch the pleats doesn't affect the fit of the garment, just its design. Unstitched pleats look a little softer.

While a pleat provides slightly more wearing ease (circumference beyond that needed to accommodate the body) than the dart it replaces, pleats don't give you license to wear a garment that's too small. If the garment is too tight, the pleats will pull open unattractively.

Like a dart, a pleat has an angle and an end point, even though the legs of a pleat are not stitched to the endpoint. The pleat, like the dart, must aim toward the apex, but, unlike a dart, a pleat can extend right to the apex. The more ease there is in a garment, the more leeway you have in how far from the apex the pleat can point. In a moderately fitted garment (like the blouse in the photo), a

Dart basics and dressmakers' vs. patternmakers' darts

Before you can manipulate darts (including turning darts into pleats), you must understand how they work. Bust darts release fabric over the bust, while holding it in where it's not needed—at the waist, for example. This dart's width is determined by the difference between the bust and waist measurements: with a 35-in. bust and 25-in. waist, for example, there are 10 in. that need to be taken up by darts. The rules regarding darts are that they must originate at a seam; must end at or near the apex (the apex is the fullest part of any body curve, whether it's the breast, hip bone, or buttock); and must be the proper width. (For a thorough discussion of darts, see *Threads* No. 35, p. 45; and No. 14, p. 64.)

In addition, you need to understand that the darts in your commercial patterns are *dressmakers' darts*, and before you can relocate them, you must change these darts into *patternmakers' darts*. A patternmakers' dart is drawn to the apex. But if the dart were sewn to the apex, the garment would have zero wearing ease. A dressmakers' dart stops ½ in. to 2 in. short of the apex to give the garment the needed wearing ease. (The exception is in garments where a very tight fit is desired, such as a cocktail dress, where the dart is sewn to within ½ in. of the bust apex.) When patternmaking, you work with the patternmakers' dart, which uses the apex as a reference point.

To change a dressmakers' dart into a patternmakers' dart, bisect the dart and extend the line to the apex. Then redraw the legs of the dart to the apex (or to the level of the apex, if the dart doesn't aim directly at the apex), as shown in the drawing at right.—*J.J.*

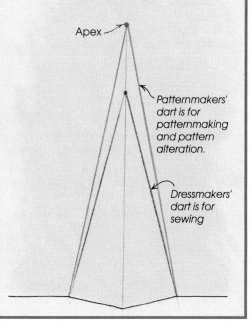

Apex

Patternmakers' dart is for patternmaking and pattern alteration.

Dressmakers' dart is for sewing

Widening a pleat

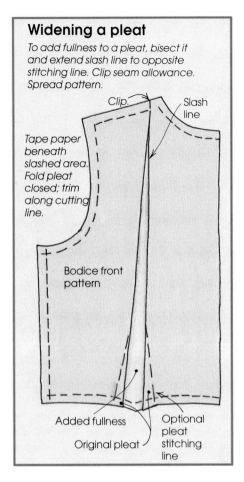

To add fullness to a pleat, bisect it and extend slash line to opposite stitching line. Clip seam allowance. Spread pattern.

Clip

Slash line

Tape paper beneath slashed area. Fold pleat closed; trim along cutting line.

Bodice front pattern

Added fullness

Original pleat

Optional pleat stitching line

pleat can even bypass the apex by 2 or 3 in. But if the pleat's endpoint is too far from the apex, unsightly pulls and wrinkles will result. In a fitted garment there is very little leeway; the pleat must aim toward the apex and end near it.

Sometimes a pleat that is just wide enough to replace a dart looks skimpy; a more generous pleat tends to look richer. The drawing at left shows how to widen a pleat.

Fabric

Prints can be tricky or wonderful for pleats, depending on the particular design. Before choosing a boldly patterned (including striped or plaid) fabric, drape it on yourself to see how pleats look. Thick, spongy, or bulky fabrics are risky for pleats; they can stand out stiffly, adding unflattering bulk to your figure. However, they may be suitable for soft, unpressed pleats, and putting the pleats on the bias may help.

Having chosen a fabric, experiment with it by pinning some pleats at different widths and at different angles to the fabric grain and draping the fabric on yourself. Depending on the fabric, bias pleats can lie beautifully or sag unattractively. Pleats that align with the cross-

wise grain will stand out more stiffly than those on the lengthwise grain. Also fold the pleat underlays in one direction, then the other—which way looks best? Determine the best pleat location and direction for your figure and the fabric.

Construction

After you've relocated darts on a pattern and turned them into pleats, you'll undoubtedly need to fine-tune the pleats to accommodate your body's secondary curves and hollows and achieve a flattering look. Always make a sample garment—a muslin—using an inexpensive fabric of a similar weight and drape. Allow 1½-in. seam allowances for any seam with pleats so that in case you need to reposition the pleats, you will have enough fabric for the seam allowance of the pleat underlays.

Cut your fashion fabric as well with 1½-in. seam allowances to allow further adjustments. Assemble the garment, pinning the seams that contain pleats from the outside where they'll be accessible for easy adjustment. Then try on the garment. If the pleats don't lie smoothly, unpin and fiddle with them until they do, then repin. After your pleats are perfect, mark the seamlines and seam allow-

Rotating waist darts to shoulder

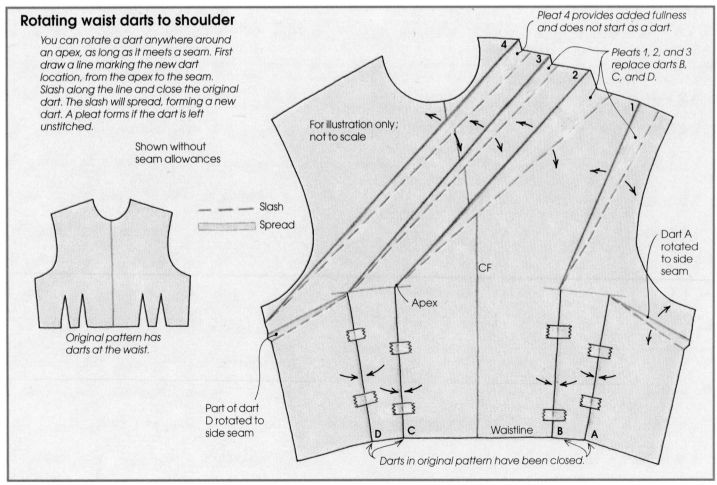

You can rotate a dart anywhere around an apex, as long as it meets a seam. First draw a line marking the new dart location, from the apex to the seam. Slash along the line and close the original dart. The slash will spread, forming a new dart. A pleat forms if the dart is left unstitched.

Shown without seam allowances

- - - - Slash

▭ Spread

Original pattern has darts at the waist.

Pleat 4 provides added fullness and does not start as a dart.

4
3
2
1

Pleats 1, 2, and 3 replace darts B, C, and D.

For illustration only; not to scale

CF

Apex

Dart A rotated to side seam

Part of dart D rotated to side seam

D C

Waistline

B A

Darts in original pattern have been closed.

ances, then cut away excess fabric.

Press this type of pleat lightly, especially pleats that go across the bias. Hard pressing will stretch them out of shape.

Asymmetrical pleated blouse

To illustrate the process of turning darts into pleats, I'll explain how you can transform a basic darted blouse pattern into a totally different blouse that has pleats. The basic process can be applied to any darted blouse that fits you. I started with Simplicity pattern 9412 and created the asymmetrical blouse with shoulder pleats shown in the photo on p. 36. But you needn't start with this particular pattern, or even a similar one.

Because I planned an asymmetrical design, with the closure at one shoulder, I needed full front and full back pattern pieces. If your design is symmetrical, you can work with the half pattern pieces.

Determining the location of the pleats— Pin the front and back pattern pieces together at sides and shoulders. Put on a leotard or a formfitting undergarment that you can pin to. Standing in front of a mirror, check that the side seams are perpendicular to the floor, and pin the pattern to your leotard at the shoulders and centers. Then hold your fabric up to yourself in front of the mirror; drape and tuck it across the pattern to find the most attractive placement and width for pleats. At this point you're just roughly locating the pleats on the pattern and checking their proportions. When they look right, pin the pleats through both the pattern and your leotard. (Pinning to the leotard prevents the pattern paper from tearing.) Gingerly step out of your leotard, leaving everything pinned together, and then detach the leotard from the pattern and fabric. Mark the pleat locations on your pattern, and write down the pleat widths. Finally, unpin the fabric from the pattern.

Moving darts— If you want your pleated blouse to have the same amount of ease as your darted pattern, you'll transform darts into pleats by drawing pleat lines to the dart endpoints. This is just basic dart manipulation and does not provide any extra fullness. I first did my blouse this way because I was curious to see what it would look like with minimal added fullness. The lower right-hand drawing on the facing page shows what that pattern looked like. I knew that when I tried on the muslin, I'd have the option of adding fullness, if I desired.

First change the darts on your pattern to patternmakers' darts. My pattern had

two darts on each side of the front, so I redrew the darts to the level of my apex, not to the apex itself. I wanted to leave just a little bust shaping in darts, so I first rotated dart A to the side seam.

For pleat 1, I drew a line from the pleat location I had marked on the pattern at the shoulder to the endpoint of dart B. I slashed on that line, then cut out and taped shut dart B, thereby opening the pattern to form pleat 1. I used the same method to transform dart C into pleat 2.

I handled dart D differently. I wanted an underarm dart on the right side to mirror the one on the left. I shifted most of dart D into pleat 3, but saved just a little to make a small underarm dart. Pleat 4 is simply extra fullness; it's not based on a dart at all. To make it, I slashed the pattern to the side seamline, then spread the pattern open.

Checking the pattern changes— Checking a design in real fabric is an important part of the process. I don't recommend ever cutting your fashion fabric until you've tried on a sample garment and fine-tuned your design. So after I trued the pattern, I sewed and tried on a muslin. My design had no closure except at the shoulder, and I was hoping the blouse

was loose enough to pull on over my shoulders. It was, but just barely!

I studied the muslin in the mirror. The size and location of the pleats did indeed provide enough fullness to replace the bust darts, but the pleats didn't look quite right. What had looked pleasing on paper did not look pleasing on my body. (This is why it's critical to make a muslin when you've made any significant pattern changes!) The pleats were too skimpy; I felt they were about half as deep as they should have been.

The solution was to widen the pleats I had already made, applying the technique shown in the top left drawing on the facing page. The drawing on this page shows the results. Before a pleat can be widened, it must extend to a seam. Pleat 4 already extended to the side seam, so I simply spread it wider. I extended pleat 3 to the side seam and redirected pleat 2 to the waist seam, then spread them both wider. I left pleat 1 alone. After making these pattern changes, I made a new muslin, and it looked great. The pleats draped softly diagonally across the bodice.   □

Jann Jasper, formerly a patternmaker in New York City's fashion industry, is a freelance writer in Ann Arbor, MI.

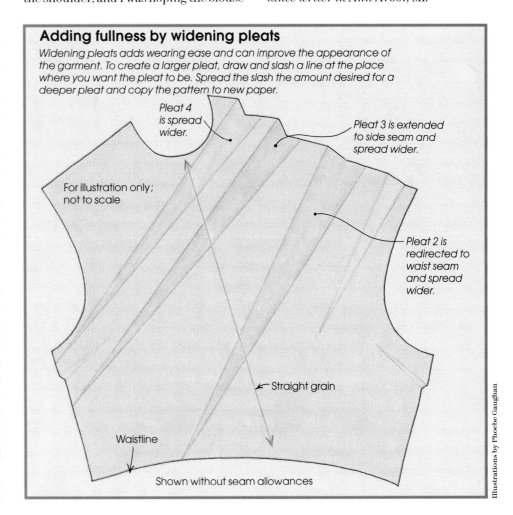

Adding fullness by widening pleats

Widening pleats adds wearing ease and can improve the appearance of the garment. To create a larger pleat, draw and slash a line at the place where you want the pleat to be. Spread the slash the amount desired for a deeper pleat and copy the pattern to new paper.

Pleat 4 is spread wider.

Pleat 3 is extended to side seam and spread wider.

For illustration only; not to scale

Pleat 2 is redirected to waist seam and spread wider.

← Straight grain

Waistline

Shown without seam allowances

Illustrations by Phoebe Gaughan

Sleeve Finesse

The Yin and Yang of armholes and sleeve caps

by Jann Jasper

The currently stylish deep armhole has wrinkles under the arm but allows more freedom of arm movement. The original sleeve (on mannequin) is smoother when the arm hangs at the side. (Photo by Susan Kahn)

Perhaps you'd like to redesign the sleeve on a commercial pattern. Maybe you're making your own patterns from a custom sloper and want to deepen the armhole. Or you may have a favorite pattern that you want to reuse, but the high armhole feels tight and looks old-fashioned. Whether you're designing a pattern or just altering an old jacket, you need to know how sleeves and armholes work, and why, or you can be in for some nasty surprises.

Designing sleeve styles in their infinite variety is easy; the tricky part is fitting the armhole and sleeve cap—a beautiful sleeve style can be ruined if it isn't fitted well. When the armhole is involved, even a seemingly simple alteration is usually more complicated than it appears.

Sleeve types

Sleeves are tricky because they must permit arm movement, yet look smooth and attractive when your arms are at rest at your sides. The degree to which sleeves succeed at this balancing act is determined primarily by the shaping (or lack thereof) provided by their underarm seams.

All sleeves fall into two categories: those with curved underarm seams that provide this shaping and those without. Sleeves with curved underarm seams, such as set-in sleeves and some raglans, allow freedom of arm movement without unattractive underarm wrinkling. Sleeves without curved underarm seams, like kimono, dolman, T, and cap sleeves (in sewing terms, a kimono sleeve is any square, unshaped sleeve, usually cut in one with the bodice), wrinkle under the arm. To succeed, these styles

must be deep and dramatic or very short. If the sleeve is long and also fitted, inclusion of an underarm gusset sidesteps this problem, as in the fitted cut-in-one sleeves on some dresses from the 1950s.

Don't be misled by the mere presence of an underarm seam, however. Not all such seams actually perform a shaping function; many are merely style features. Some raglan sleeves are, in terms of construction and fit, actually kimono sleeves with an essentially decorative diagonal seam. If you lay the armhole seam of the sleeve pattern against the armhole seam of the bodice pattern and the edges dovetail together with little or no gap, there is no underarm shaping, the seam is decorative, and the sleeve will have underarm wrinkles.

Opportunities for refining the appearance and fit of sleeves without underarm shaping are limited. Therefore, I'll focus on sleeves with underarm shaping. For clarity, I'll use set-in sleeves as examples, but the principles apply to raglan sleeves as well.

Three key factors

For a comfortable, attractive armhole and sleeve—one that doesn't bind or cut into the armpit, that permits free arm movement, and that has a relatively smooth appearance while the arm is at rest—three factors must come together: The armhole must be the right shape, the armhole must be the right depth, and the sleeve cap must be shaped properly. There are many "right" solutions, depending on the garment style and your comfort requirements. The three factors are interdependent—most changes in the bodice armhole require corresponding changes in the sleeve cap—but you must understand each factor independently. Once you do, you can manipulate them to create any style you want in a sleeve that fits.

Armhole shape—The pattern shape of a front armhole is different from that of the back, on both the bodice and sleeve. This difference is based on anatomy: The front armhole is scooped deeper to allow for forward arm movement. The back scoop is shallower because backward arm movement is infrequent and limited. The lengths are also different: The back armhole is longer to accommodate the body's convex curve over the shoulder blades; the body curve in front is concave due to the hollow in front of the shoulder socket. You can see these differences by laying the front bodice of some of your patterns over the back and by folding the sleeves in half lengthwise. (This is also a good way to distinguish front from back.)

The armhole shape must be correct before you can make changes to the sleeve cap. For example, if a garment feels tight when you move your arms forward, it may be because the back armhole has been scooped too much, and so there isn't enough width across the bodice back. If the problem is in the bodice, trying to fix it in the sleeve cap is futile.

The shape of a very loose armhole is less crucial than that of a high, fitted armhole because the armhole doesn't cup the body's arm-shoulder joint. For example, in a stylized, deep armhole the curves are shallow. The top drawing compares a high, fitted armhole with a deep, loose one.

Armhole depth—There's a widespread misconception that a deep armhole gives more comfort and freedom of movement than a high one. Nothing could be farther from the truth. By itself, a deep armhole limits arm movement; when you lift your arm, the whole garment is dragged up with the

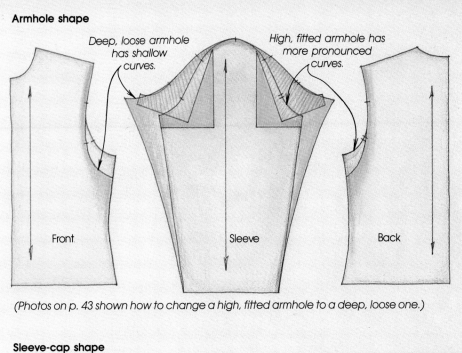

Armhole shape

Deep, loose armhole has shallow curves.

High, fitted armhole has more pronounced curves.

Front

Sleeve

Back

(Photos on p. 43 shown how to change a high, fitted armhole to a deep, loose one.)

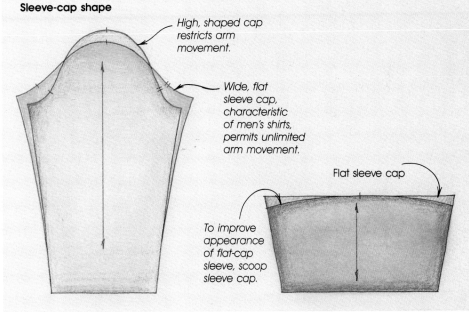

Sleeve-cap shape

High, shaped cap restricts arm movement.

Wide, flat sleeve cap, characteristic of men's shirts, permits unlimited arm movement.

Flat sleeve cap

To improve appearance of flat-cap sleeve, scoop sleeve cap.

sleeve. If a style also has a fitted waist, lifting the arm will be difficult. European clothes have high-cut armholes that many of us find more comfortable than clothes with deep armholes. Even when made of stretch fabric, active sportswear has very high armholes that actually cup the shoulder socket to permit maximum arm movement. If you're unconvinced, picture the underarm of your shirt ripping open when you lift your arm. The resulting gap between armhole and sleeve shows you exactly what's needed to increase freedom of arm movement: more length in the underarm.

The minimum armhole depth is 1½ in. below the armpit. To measure the minimum armhole size you need for comfort in a blouse of woven fabric, wear a leotard and place a pencil tight up under your arm. Mark a point 1½ in. below the pencil; this is the armhole depth and the top of the side seam of the bodice. Then form a circle with a measuring tape, holding it closed between your forefinger and your thumb. Stick your arm through and pull the tape up to your shoulder joint, placing the top of the circle at the end of the shoulder seam/shoulder point. Let your arm hang down loosely. Adjust the size of the tape circle until its bottom reaches the 1½-in. mark. Fasten the tape shut, and note the measurement of the circumference. Check this measurement against that of a comfortable blouse; it's easy to measure yourself too tightly the first time.

Sleeve-cap shape—There's no one sleeve-cap shape that's right for every garment. Sleeves designed for appearance have high, shaped caps that are wrinkle-free when the

Making room for shoulder pads

Football-player-sized shoulder pads are out of fashion, but more moderate pads continue to be worn. Many women remain loyal to shoulder pads because by extending the shoulders, the pads visually reduce the waistline. They're also useful to disguise figure flaws. And I doubt we'll ever see a woman's business suit without them.

Shoulder pads come in styles for raglan, set-in, and cap sleeves, and in many thicknesses. Some are washable; some must be dry-cleaned. If a garment with pads has wrinkles, it's because the wrong style or size pad has been used (never use a set-in pad for a raglan garment, or vice versa) or because pattern adjustments weren't made to the shoulder and sleeve to accommodate the pad.

If you buy the size your pattern calls for, you don't need to change anything.

Adjusting for shoulder pads

Raise shoulder seam at sleeve by thickness of pad (half on front bodice, half on back). Extend shoulder slightly.

Half thickness of shoulder pad

Front and back bodices

Thickness of shoulder pad

Sleeve

Slash and spread sleeve cap by thickness of shoulder pad.

But if you want to use larger or smaller pads, remove them, or add them where they weren't specified. Both the bodice and the sleeve must be adjusted.

To accommodate shoulder pads in a pattern that doesn't call for them, you must raise the shoulder seam, at the sleeve, to make room for the pad (see drawing at left). The amount you add to the shoulder is the thickness of the pad: Half goes on the bodice-front shoulder seam and half on the bodice-back shoulder seam. You can play it safe by adding a bit more, and you can trim off excess after trying on the garment.

Next, because shoulder pads are always positioned to extend beyond the natural shoulder hinge, extend the shoulder width by $\frac{1}{4}$ in. for a small pad, up to $\frac{5}{8}$ in. for a large pad.

Make corresponding changes to the sleeve. To lengthen the sleeve cap to fit the enlarged armhole created by raising the shoulder, slash and spread the pattern as shown. —J.J.

---

arms are at the side, but they restrict arm movement, as in most evening wear for women. At the other extreme, sleeves designed for action have flatter, wider caps; e.g., those on active sportswear, uniforms, and mens' shirts. The bottom drawing on p. 41 shows these two types of caps.

Until recently, women's sleeves have been much more confining than men's, the difference being mainly in sleeve-cap shape. In the past several years, the high, shaped cap characteristic of women's sleeves has been replaced by a more relaxed style, which we now take for granted. If you try on a dress from the '60s or '70s, you'll feel how uncomfortable the armhole and sleeve are.

Flattening the cap is the way to improve a sleeve's wearing comfort without changing the armhole depth and without significantly changing the sleeve's appearance. I refer to it as adding "lift" because it enables you to lift your arm without strain.

The drawback of the flat-cap sleeve is that it's designed for comfortable arm movement, not for a smooth look when your arm is at rest. To understand this trade-off, move your arm up from your side to a horizontal position, then to above your head. If you provide enough fabric to lift your arm really high, the fabric will wrinkle when your arm is at rest. The wrinkles emanate from the underarm, and the sleeve also pokes out at the top, a characteristic you often see in T-shirts and sportswear. It's possible to improve the appearance of a flat-cap sleeve somewhat, in the pattern stage or sometimes even on a finished garment, by slightly scooping a square sleeve cap (bottom drawing, p. 41).

While the lift principle always holds true, adding lift isn't always necessary or desirable. If the garment is loose throughout the back, you can lift your arm even in a high-cap sleeve because you're borrowing from the fabric in the body circumference— the whole bodice may lift up when you raise your arm—or if the sleeve is loose or short, added lift isn't needed. But if the garment is fitted or has a tightly belted waist or the sleeve is long and fitted or cuffed, more sleeve lift is needed.

Although you can increase arm movement in a high-cap sleeve by flattening the sleeve cap somewhat without deepening the armhole, the reverse is not true; you can't deepen the armhole without also flattening the sleeve cap (unless you're willing to lose some arm movement). This is because deepening the armhole takes away fabric that you need to lift your arm, and unless you compensate by adding to the underarm part of the sleeve, it has the effect of binding your arms to your sides. If you doubt this, safety-pin the sleeve seam of a blouse to the side seam 1 in. below the armhole, try on the blouse, and see how far you can lift your arm without lifting the entire blouse up with it.

Ease

The ease in a sleeve cap has more to do with sewing than with patternmaking and fitting because different fabrics have different characteristics. The three primary factors that determine sleeve comfort are far more important than ease when it comes to getting a good fit and must be corrected before ease can be adjusted.

The sleeve cap has ease added to give it a smooth, rounded appearance and to accommodate the curve of the upper arm. Ease is obtained when the sleeve cap is made longer than the armhole that it will be set into. The amount of ease needed is dictated partly by garment style, with the most ease found in coat and jacket sleeves and high-cap sleeves. At the other extreme, flat-cap sport-shirt sleeves, with their built-in room to move, have little, if any, added ease. For the same reason, full or gathered sleeve styles don't need any ease, and ease is usually eliminated in knits.

The standard amounts of ease built into sleeve caps are $\frac{1}{4}$ in. to $1\frac{1}{2}$ in. for a blouse or dress, and $1\frac{1}{2}$ in. to 2 in. for a jacket or coat. The pattern's armhole notches correspond to the beginning of the body's underarm curve. The sleeve measurement below the notches matches that of the armhole. Above the notches the sleeve is bigger, and the difference is the ease.

Easing is a process of compressing and shrinking the fabric with the iron. Therefore, fabric properties also dictate the amount of ease suitable for a given style; some fabrics are difficult, if not impossible, to ease and shouldn't be used for some styles. Synthetics don't ease well; they don't shrink, and they can't take heat. Malleable, loose weaves ease better than stiff, firm weaves. Permanent-press fabrics don't ease well.

Application to your patterns

I've explained these aspects of sleeves separately to make them clear, but they operate together; e.g., a deep armhole is also less curved than a high one because it's not in-

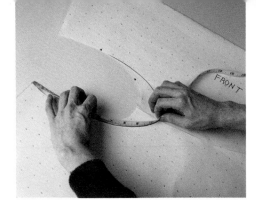

Photos by Mary Galpin Barnes

Making a flatter sleeve and a deeper armhole: *Measure the new armhole (and the old) by standing a tape measure on edge (top, left). Slash and spread, lifting the sleeve underarm by the amount you deepened the armhole (bottom, left). After extending the sleeve cap by the amount you lengthened the armhole, taper the new sleeve seam to the wrist, using a curved ruler (above). Then smooth out the sleeve cap, eliminating the peaks at the base of the armhole.*

volved in shoulder-joint movement. And it requires a flatter sleeve cap to permit arm movement. A high, shaped cap with a high armhole yields a smooth sleeve that allows moderate arm movement, but the look is dated; flattening the cap would increase arm movement. A garment with a high, shaped cap with a deep armhole would restrict arm movement a lot. A deep armhole with a wide, fairly flat cap will allow movement but will have wrinkles under the arm.

To illustrate how to incorporate some of these principles, I'll explain the procedure of *deepening the armhole and flattening the sleeve cap* on a sample pattern. The photos above show the procedure. You can make this adjustment to reuse an old pattern that has tight, high armholes; to increase the arm movement of a fitted garment in a new pattern; or to deepen the armhole of a custom sloper.

1. Trace the bodice and sleeve patterns onto plain or pattern paper, eliminating seam allowances. Mark the new, lower armhole depth on both front and back bodices. I've made it 2 in. deeper, a significant change.

Lay the front and back bodice pattern pieces side seam to side seam so you can visualize the new armhole curve. Draw new curves to the lower armhole depth, repositioning a French curve until you arrive at smooth shapes. Remember that the back curve is shallower than the front, but since you're deepening the armhole, both curves will be shallower than they originally were.

Measure the old and new armhole lengths by standing a tape measure on edge (1). The difference between them is the amount you've lengthened the armhole.

2. Flatten the sleeve cap. You can't just trim off the cap to flatten it, as this would shorten the finished sleeve length. Instead, you must lift the underarm by slashing and lifting the sleeve-underarm area.

Draw a horizontal slash line on the sleeve about 1 in. below the base of the armhole and two vertical slash lines about 2 in. to each side of the shoulder-seam notch. Cut along the lines, leaving intact the center portion of the horizontal line and a tiny section of paper at the top of each of the vertical slash lines to serve as pivot points. Lay the slashed sleeve on a large, new sheet of paper, taping down only the center portion. Extend the horizontal line beyond the sleeve seam.

3. Lift (spread) the slashed segments by at least the amount that you deepened the armhole (in my case, 2 in.), measured from the base of the armhole to the extended horizontal line (2). The more you spread, the more underarm folds you'll get. Tape down the triangular sections. Blend the new sleeve-cap line smoothly with pencil and curves, eliminating the peaks at the base of the armhole.

4. Make the new sleeve fit the new armhole by lengthening the cap by the amount that you lengthened the armhole (the difference in length between the old armhole and the new armhole from step 1): Extend the cap at each side by half this amount. Taper the new sleeve seam to the wrist, curving the line to give a pleasing shape to the sleeve (3). To duplicate the sleeve-seam curve on the other side, fold over the paper lengthwise, matching the end points of the sleeve seams. (To match, stick one pin

through both end points at the wrist and another through the end points at the armhole.) Cut both sleeve seams together along the curve.

Double-check your work by comparing the new sleeve-cap measurement with the new armhole measurement: The cap length should be the measurement of the armhole, plus the amount of ease you want. You need less ease for a flatter cap; a totally flat-cap sleeve may have no ease at all.

Correct the notches. Move the lower ones on the front and back bodice armholes across to the new armhole curve, maintaining the same positions. Measure from side seam to notch on the bodice-front armhole and mark the lower notch on the sleeve front this distance from the sleeve seam. Repeat for the back. If your sleeve has a second set of notches (as mine does), maintain the original distances between the notches on both armhole and sleeve cap. Measure the length of the armscye on the bodice front. Mark a small dot on the sleeve cap this distance from the sleeve seam. Repeat for the back. Position the shoulder-seam notch on the sleeve cap midway between these two points to distribute the ease evenly between front and back. Add seam allowances. Trim excess paper.

The first few times you make these pattern changes, test them in muslin. Once you understand the principles, you'll find that they're not hard to make, and a whole new world of sleeves will be opened to you.□

Jann Jasper, a patternmaker and freelance writer in New York City, is a frequent contributor to Threads.

Narrowing a Sleeve
A more comfortable fit plus fabric savings

by Margaret Komives

One of the current design trends in patterns is the undarted bodice with deep armholes and very full sleeves. These lines are pleasing to the eye and comfortable to wear as a dress or blouse without a jacket, or as a coat over a garment of similar cut.

But let's face it—who needs all that sleeve, especially if the garment is to be worn under a vest, a semi-fitted jacket, or a coat? Not only will the fabric get badly wrinkled, but the comfort level will surely be low with that excess fabric gathered up at the underarm.

And who needs the inconvenience? These sleeves are often more than 22½ in. wide, which means that you would have to cut one piece, then refold the fabric at least once more, often twice, to cut the remaining pieces. It is nothing short of a logistics problem to keep the fabric on grain with all this refolding, especially if the fabric is one of the lovely silkies we all like to use.

Check out the pattern layout

A full-sleeve design is not always fully evident from the diagram or the photo on the pattern envelope. Many stores will allow you to take the guide sheet out of the pattern envelope before purchasing it. That way you can study the pattern piece diagrams and the layout. If you see, on a 45-in. layout, that half the fabric width does not accommodate the sleeve pattern, you know that the sleeve is cut very full.

If you really like the pattern otherwise, the sleeves can be easily adjusted. The higher armhole that results will likely be more comfortable. And the change can result in considerable savings. The last blouse pattern I used called for 2⅞ yds. of fabric. By slightly narrowing the sleeve, I was able to cut the blouse from just under 2¼ yds., a ⅝-yd. savings. Not having to refold the fabric and reestablish the grainline was also a real savings of time and effort, to say nothing of my sanity.

Tuck out the pattern

Measuring and tucking excess out of a sleeve pattern is a simple procedure. And you can always reuse the adjusted pattern. To show you how it's done, I've adjusted two types of pattern: one with a standard set-in sleeve and one with a raglan sleeve.

Adjusting a set-in sleeve—For the standard set-in sleeve top, make the first correction to the sleeve pattern. Lay it on the fabric, which is folded in half on the lengthwise grain, to see how much will have to be removed. Let's say it's 2 in. That means we'll take 1 in. out of each half of each sleeve. These sleeves usually have a very shallow cap, so it's no problem to remove the excess width: Fold two ½-in.-deep tucks, each of which takes up 1 in. of the pattern width, parallel to the grainline, beginning about midway between the center of the cap and the underarm seam, as shown at top on the facing page. Try to avoid the area with the greatest slant. True the cutting line (see *Basics, Threads* No. 34 for more on tucking, slashing and spreading) and the seamline.

Next, take out 1 in. from the bodice front and back in the armscye area by folding a ½-in.-deep tuck perpendicular to the grainline, again avoiding the area of greatest slant. We have to compromise on position in this example because of a special placket; we make the tuck just below it. If there is a separate facing piece, make the same alteration on it.

Whatever amount is removed from the length of a garment in the armscye area must be added at the lengthen-or-shorten line or the lower edge if the length is to remain the same. Slash on the lengthen-or-shorten line and spread the pattern (1 in.). The blouse will be the same length it was originally.

One last detail: The sleeve is attached to a cuff. Hence, the original width at the lower edge must be restored by adding to the un-

For a better fit with overgarments, try a simple sleeve-narrowing pattern adjustment.

derarm seams. To do so, you can pivot out from the underarm/armscye cutting-line junction the needed amount (in this case 1 in.) on each side, and retrace the cutting lines. (For more on pivot-and-slide pattern adjustments, see the article on pp. 20-23).

Adjusting a raglan style—For the raglan sleeve, pattern adjustments are no more difficult, although the pattern is a bit different in that the sleeve begins at the neckline. Lay out the sleeve pattern, as explained above, to see how much the sleeve should be narrowed to accommodate the fabric. If that amount gives you the desired armscye height, you're all set. Simply tuck out the excess on the sleeve and on the bodice, then lengthen the bodice to compensate, just as you would for a set-in sleeve.

On some raglan styles, you may want to raise the armhole even more, without narrowing the sleeve further than would be necessary for an economical fabric layout. It's actually easy to do (photos, lower right). I planned to make a blouse to wear with a handknit sweater-vest that has a deep armhole, but not nearly as deep as the sleeve pattern. While I found that I would need to narrow the sleeve by 1½ in., I wanted to shorten the armscye 2 in. to match the vest. I narrowed the sleeve the needed 1½ in. by tucking out ¾ in. from each side parallel to the grainline. Then I shortened the bodice armscye by tucking out the desired 2 in. front and back, perpendicular to the grainline, in the flattest part of the armhole curve. That left 1¼ in. still to be removed from each side of the sleeve armscye, which I accomplished with a crosswise tuck (photo, right). Thus on one-half of the sleeve I removed ¾ in. from the width and 1¼ in. from the length, for a total of 2 in. A larger lengthwise tuck would have distorted the raglan seamline angle too much. This way, it's easy to true the armscye lines.

Our crosswise tuck in the sleeve actually shortens it, so we make a corresponding slash, and spread the sleeve pattern as well as the bodice pattern, at the lengthen-or-shorten line. We also widen the sleeve at the bottom to match up with the cuff.

There is very little apparent change in the resulting garments, yet we've made cutting simpler and more economical, and the garments more versatile. Try it on the next wide-sleeved, deep-armscye blouse or dress you make. You'll be delighted with the results. □

Margaret Komives writes about and teaches sewing and tailoring at the Brown Deer Center of the Milwaukee Area Technical College. She explained how to make a perfect lapel in Threads, *No. 24. (Photos by the author)*

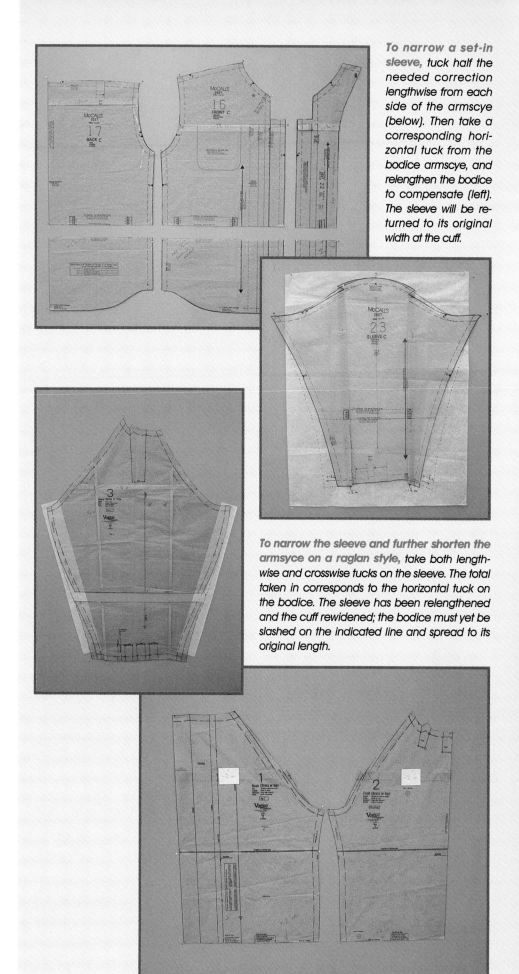

To narrow a set-in sleeve, tuck half the needed correction lengthwise from each side of the armscye (below). Then take a corresponding horizontal tuck from the bodice armscye, and relengthen the bodice to compensate (left). The sleeve will be returned to its original width at the cuff.

To narrow the sleeve and further shorten the armsyce on a raglan style, take both lengthwise and crosswise tucks on the sleeve. The total taken in corresponds to the horizontal tuck on the bodice. The sleeve has been relengthened and the cuff rewidened; the bodice must yet be slashed on the indicated line and spread to its original length.

Shoulder Pads—In or Out?

How to achieve a flattering shoulder shape regardless of the current style

by Jan Larkey

Shoulder pads have been in fashion now for more than ten years, far longer than the typical fashion trend, which usually lasts around five years; mere fads are generally played out in two years. Why have shoulder pads endured for so long? The obvious answer is that they help people look better. But lately fashion seems to be trying to convince us that we're tired of shoulder pads, even the more natural ones of the past several years. Before you decide to give yours up, let's consider the figure advantages most of us have enjoyed during the previous, padded decade.

Our shoulder area is a very visible part of our figures, especially when we are seated behind a table or desk. Drooping shoulders can send a message that we are tired or discouraged when we actually feel great. A more positive set to our shoulders sends a message of confidence. Even a small, naturally shaped shoulder pad can help our clothes look and fit better. Sloping or rounded shoulders, for example, cause garments to hang with unattractive creases through the bodice, and are easily visually corrected with pads. And last, but certainly not least, wider shoulders visually balance wide hips.

Figure out your shoulders

To determine what to wear to make the most of your own figure, I suggest you first analyze how your figure varies from classic idealized proportions. Is it wide where it would ideally be narrow, protruding where it ought to be flat? Then use the style lines (like seams, lapels, waistbands, hems, prominent details, and so on) and the silhouette of your clothing to create the illusion that your figure *has* more ideal proportions. For example, vertical lines on garments direct a viewer's eye up and down, so if you want to make some part of your body look longer and narrower than it actually is, wear vertical lines there; conversely, wear horizontal lines where you want to suggest width. Use shoulder pads, which actually change your silhouette, as well as garment style lines and details to suggest a more ideal shoulder shape which will enhance your entire figure.

The classic ideal for shoulders is that

Do your hips balance your shoulders?

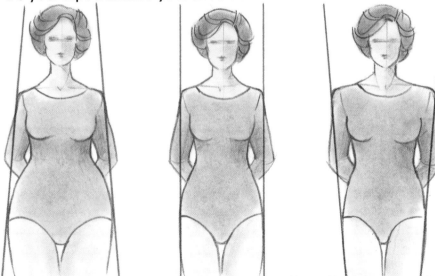

Ideally, shoulders are as wide as, or slightly wider than, hips. Have a friend place one end of a yardstick or dowel at your shoulder point, then rest the other end at the widest part of the hip/thigh area. If the stick is perfectly vertical, your hips and shoulders are balanced.

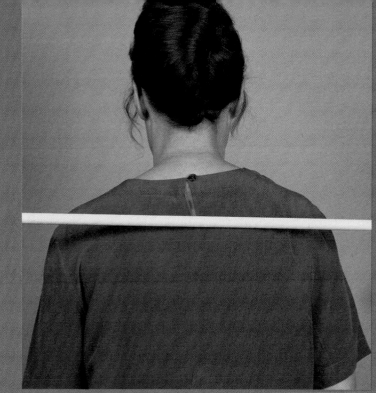

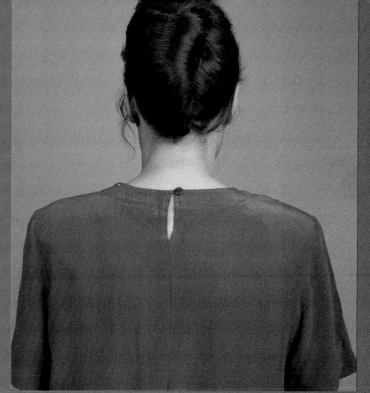

To see the shape of your shoulders (left), have a friend hold a dowel horizontally across your shoulders, front or back. The slope, and any unevenness, will be immediately apparent.

Carefully chosen pads, in this case one large and one small, can usually compensate for excessive slope and an uneven shoulder line, without creating an overstuffed or unnatural look.

they be as wide as or slightly wider than the hips. They should also be neither too sloping nor too square, nor too round or undefined, and of course they should be level. As with all ideals, very few people exemplify them, but it's not hard to create the illusion that you do.

Shoulders are easy to analyze for shape and proportion, but it can help to use a simple device to check how they relate to the hips, the degree of slope, and whether they're even or not. A plain dowel or yard stick held simultaneously against the hip and the shoulder point on one side, as in the drawing on the facing page, will quickly tell whether the shoulders are wider, balanced, or narrower than the hips. Held horizontally at shoulder level, as in the left-hand photo above, the dowel shows immediately that my shoulders are uneven, as well as quite sloped.

Finding solutions

Common shoulder shapes are sloping, uneven, and narrow; extra wide; and rounded or full. Let's discuss flattering garment choices for each situation.

Sloping, narrow, or uneven shoulders— These situations don't necessarily come hand in hand, but their solutions are similar, so I'm lumping them together. If you fall into any of these categories, I advise you to wear shoulder pads with everything! A slight slope is natural for shoul-

ders, but generally speaking, the squarer the better. One thick and one thin shoulder pad provided a quick and sure solution to my sloping shoulders, and evened them out as well, as you can see in the right-hand photo above. If you have sloping shoulders, be aware of the slope of any horizontal style line at or near the shoulders. As you can see in the photos on pp. 48 and 49, the drooping stripe on my jacket emphasizes the slope of my shoulder line, and makes me look rounded and shapeless. Shoulder pads, which straighten the stripe, also add definition to my silhouette, and perk up the outfit.

Once corrected with shoulder pads, sloping or uneven shoulders almost cease to be a problem. You can help out further, and deal with narrow shoulders as well, by avoiding garments that emphasize shoulder shape or that have sloping style lines at the shoulder, like those with raglan, kimono, or bat-wing sleeves. You should also watch out for thick turtleneck or cowl necklines, which fill in and shorten the shoulder line. Instead, gravitate towards more defined shapes like petal, puffed, peasant, or padded-cap sleeves; epaulets; wide, flat collars; peaknotched lapels; square necklines; and Western, horizontal yokes. Vertical style lines, like pleats falling from the shoulders (see the left-hand photo on p. 48), camouflage shoulder slope. Naturally, as with any shoulder problem that calls for

pads and other disguises, avoid styles that expose the shoulders. In fact, I always wear double shoulder pads, one minimal set under my blouse, and another under my jacket. That way, I can always remove my jacket without destroying the line I want.

Wide shoulders—Not many people have shoulders that are too wide; it's wide, well-shaped shoulders that pads were created to provide. If you have broad shoulders already, you can wear almost anything that doesn't exaggerate them. Beware of making your shoulders look so large that your head begins to look too small for the rest of you! Avoid heavily padded shoulders or very wide collars. Instead, look for thin shoulder pads to create shape without adding volume. Choose vertical, center-front style lines and details, like ascots and shawl collars, and diagonal lines that converge towards your neck, such as raglan sleeves. The photos at the bottom of p. 49 dramatically demonstrate the widening or narrowing effect of diagonal lines. Val has naturally wide shoulders, but they don't look wide when she wears her black halter top. The scalloped scoop neck emphasizes the width. In neither case do her strong shoulders become a problem, but if you decide that your shoulders are too wide, avoid all the styles recommended above for narrow shoulders. Dolman and

To camouflage narrow, sloping, or uneven shoulders, choose a pattern such as McCall's 6130 that combines shoulder pleats, pads, and dolman sleeves. The extra fabric volume and a floral print add to the illusion of more ideal shoulders.

Horizontal design lines at or near the shoulders reinforce the shape and slope of the shoulders, as illustrated by the drooping line on this jacket.

kimono sleeves can be a problem here, too, because they add volume to the size of the shoulders.

Large, round shoulders—Too many women with full shoulders shun shoulder pads altogether. If a round shoulder is combined with a full upper arm, the resulting curves may appear heavier than necessary in many styles. As you can see in the top right-hand photo on the facing page, adding a shaped pad that replaces the curve with a "corner" will actually slim the shoulder and arm area. Hold your hand over each side of the picture in turn to compare the effect. On the left, Jan's curved shoulder and arm lines visually add extra weight. On the right, a shoulder pad with a slight "corner" lifts and extends the shoulder corner slightly beyond the curved natural shoulder. This minimizes the fabric folds and creates a more positive shoulder shape and a slimmer-looking arm.

Choosing pads

Shoulder pads come in a wide variety of shapes, thicknesses, and sizes. The slope and size of your shoulders, the style lines of your garment, and the drape of the fabric are all part of the equation when you're choosing the appropriate ones. Here are some guidelines for making figure-flattering choices:

• The more pronounced the slope or curve of the shoulders, the thicker the pad needs to be at the shoulder end. For jacket/blouse combinations, divide the thickness you need between two thinner pads, one in your blouse, and another in your jacket.

• Heavy shoulders need a pad just thick enough to create a straighter shoulder line. They should be shaped to suggest a shoulder "corner."

• For narrow shoulders or heavy arms, extend the armhole seam beyond the actual end of the shoulder and insert a pad so that it, too, extends beyond the actual shoulder. This will allow the sleeve fabric to hang gracefully from the extended shoulder line, camouflaging heavy shoulders or arms.

• Wear rounded-edge pads under clinging, lightweight, or draping fabrics such as lightweight knits, jerseys, satins, chiffons, silks, or spandex. A soft, rounded edge also works well with sleeves that are not set in, like raglan, dolman, or kimono styles. Wear square-edge pads under heavier, crisp, or suit-weight fabrics such as denim, wools, corduroy, gabardine, and beaded or heavy sequined tops. Square-edged pads make jackets, coats, and suit-weight garments look crisp.

Shoulder-pad tips

Wear shoulder pads even with your leisure clothing, especially sweatshirts. Their bulky fabric combined with the converging seamlines from the raglan sleeves make even wide shoulders look like they are falling off your body. And don't forget to pad your bathrobe! Pads that are attached to garments with hook-and-loop tape are easily removed for dry cleaning or laundry—or replaced with another shape. Just be sure to sew the soft loop piece to the garment and the scratchy hook piece to the shoulder pad. Always store foam shoulder pads out of direct sunlight to avoid discoloration and deterioration. □

Jan Larkey is the author of Flatter Your Figure, *available in bookstores, or by mail from her at Box 8258-T, Pittsburgh, PA, 15218. She wrote about skirt lengths and pleats in* Threads *No. 41 and body proportions in* Threads *No. 34.*

Choose pads that will keep *horizontal design elements straight* or slightly raised at the ends of the shoulders to suggest a straight shoulder line.

Don't decide you can't wear shoulder pads just because your shoulders are full already. An unpadded shoulder (left side, below) reinforces the impression of roundness, while the naturally shaped pad (right side) gives a little needed angularity, and lets the sleeve drape, slimming the arm.

Diagonal lines have a powerful visual effect, narrowing the body where they converge (above left), and widening it where they diverge (above right). Wide shoulders look much more obvious when you wear a scoop, bateau, or square neckline than when you wear a halter top, even though the halter exposes the shoulders, and the other necklines conceal them.

Here are the results of your pattern-altering efforts: a becoming jacket with soft, easy-to-sew shoulders.

The No-Seam Armhole

How to eliminate the hassle of a set-in sleeve without sacrificing the fit of your jacket

by Margaret Komives

do you search the pattern catalogs for jackets without set-in sleeves just so you can avoid the challenge of setting them in? If you've ever made a raglan-, dolman-, or kimono-sleeved jacket, you know that these garments, joined front to back with a simple seam from neckline to wrist along the shoulder line, typically trade their easy construction for the contoured fit of a darted bodice and a set-in sleeve. Even if you love the look as well as the relief, you've no doubt had to admit that the underarm fit is less than ideal, if not downright shapeless.

Some of the most intriguing designer jackets to appear in the last year or so offer an exciting compromise solution. They combine the soft, easy-to-make shoulder of the raglan sleeve with the shapely fit of a princess-seamed bodice. I call this cut the princess raglan. You can see an example in the sketch by Valentino above right and my version on the facing page; the drawing below right shows the way the pattern pieces of such a jacket fit together. Other designers who've turned to this styling lately include Matsuda and Giorgio Armani. ⇨

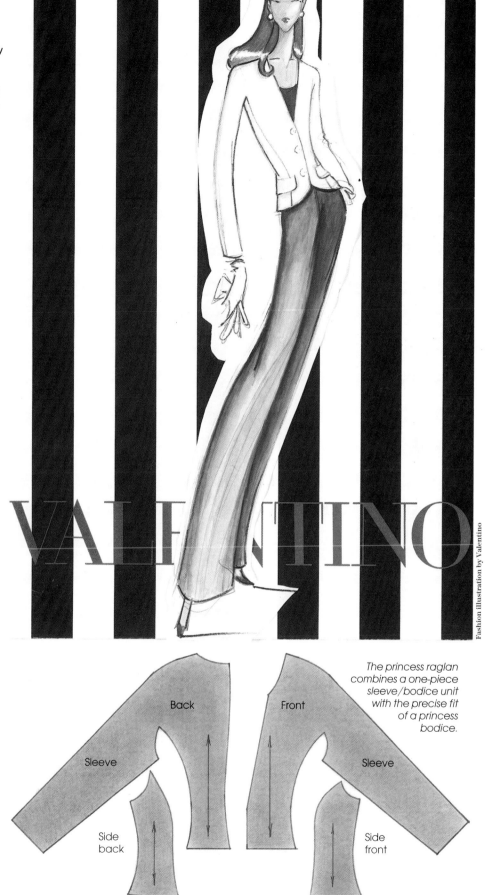

VALENTINO

Fashion illustration by Valentino

The princess raglan combines a one-piece sleeve/bodice unit with the precise fit of a princess bodice.

Back

Front

Sleeve

Sleeve

Side back

Side front

Converting a set-in-sleeve jacket to a princess raglan

To eliminate the armscye without losing the shaping the princess seam provides, you can combine the pattern pieces of a typical one-piece-sleeve, princess-seam jacket into a new pattern.

1 Trace off a copy of each major pattern piece (sleeve, front, back, sides), without seam allowances.

2 To check the position of the princess seam, measure the vertical distance from the base of the armscye to the princess seam on front and back side panels. If the distance is more than 3½ in. on either piece, redraw the princess seams to lower them, then trim off the excess and tape it to the corresponding bodice piece.

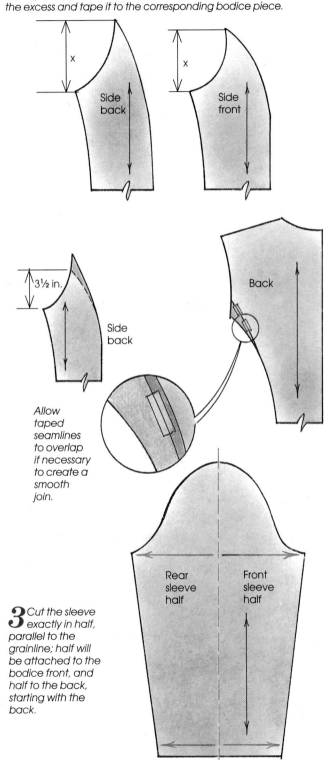

Allow taped seamlines to overlap if necessary to create a smooth join.

3 Cut the sleeve exactly in half, parallel to the grainline; half will be attached to the bodice front, and half to the back, starting with the back.

4 To mark the position of the princess seam in relation to the sleeve, lay the corrected side-back panel over the rear sleeve half, matching the ends of the armscye, and mark the end of the princess seam on the sleeve.

5 To combine the back sleeve half with the bodice back, position the rear sleeve half over the bodice back with the marked point from step 4 matching the end of princess seam, then pivot the sleeve until it forms a 45 degree angle to the grain of the bodice.

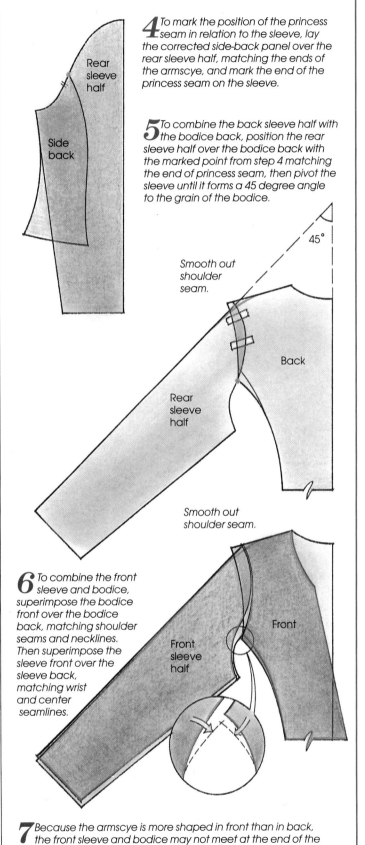

Smooth out shoulder seam.

Smooth out shoulder seam.

6 To combine the front sleeve and bodice, superimpose the bodice front over the bodice back, matching shoulder seams and necklines. Then superimpose the sleeve front over the sleeve back, matching wrist and center seamlines.

7 Because the armscye is more shaped in front than in back, the front sleeve and bodice may not meet at the end of the princess seamline. If not, pivot a short section of both seams until they meet, without changing the length of the seam.

There's every reason for home sewers to enjoy the virtues of the princess raglan, too. Besides being easier to make and to fit than jackets with set-in sleeves, its smooth, uninterrupted shoulder line is perfect for the reduced padding of the '90s, and its one-piece sleeve/bodice greatly simplifies pattern matching problems. A quick scan of the pattern catalogs reveals only one or two current examples (for instance, Vogue 2892 and 2956). More will no doubt appear as the catalogs catch up with ready-to-wear, but in fact it's surprisingly easy to convert many set-in-sleeve jacket patterns with princess seams that end in the armhole into princess raglans (see the drawings on the facing page).

In case you're thinking that it will be difficult to stitch the reverse corner near the underarm, where the princess seam turns down to become the armscye, relax. At right you'll find complete instructions for an easy method that will keep that corner looking smooth and professional in jacket-weight fabrics.

Picking a pattern to convert

Start with a basic-armhole princess-seamed jacket that has a one-piece sleeve with an underarm seam. Good examples are Butterick 6640, 6142, and 6466; McCall's 6348 and 6113; and Vogue 8601, 8612, 8598, 8251, 2637, 1766, and 2822.

It doesn't matter how your pattern is shaped below the waist (it could be cropped, extra long, peplumed, etc.) but if the cut is described as very loose, you may have to reduce the width front and back to bring the armscye more in line with your actual underarm. Check by pinning the tissue sleeve to the tissue bodice front and holding it up to your body, aligning the center front. If the armscye falls over your arm, take a vertical tuck in the bodice piece, moving the entire outer edge until the armscye sits on top of your underarm crease. Make a similar tuck in the back to keep the shoulder seams the same length. You should always make a muslin test garment when you're doing extensive alterations like this conversion, so you can check this adjustment on the muslin as well. At this point, before converting, make any pattern adjustments for fit that you would normally make.

You'll notice in drawings 1-6 on the facing page that you typically lose about an inch of the sleeve cap when you convert to a princess raglan. This isn't a problem, since most of this is ease which you don't need if you're not setting in the sleeve. ☐

Margaret Komives is a frequent contributor to Threads.

Stitching the armscye's corner

This method works well for jacket-weight fabrics because the reverse corner can be flattened before it's stitched down. Use the same method for both front and back corners.

1 Mark the corner on both bodice and side pieces with thread, carbon, or removable marker. Mark the wrong side (WS) of the bodice, and the right side (RS) of the side panel.

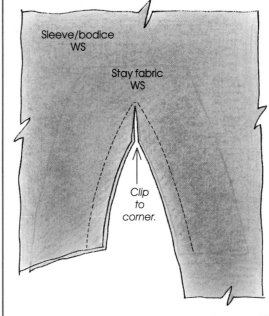

2 Place a piece of pressable, thin, strong stay fabric on the RS of the bodice corner. Then machine stitch with short stitches right next to the seamline in the seam allowance, from the WS, taking one stitch across the point at the corner. Clip to the corner through both layers. The pivot stitch allows you to clip right to the stitch and still have a tiny seam allowance.

3 Turn stay fabric to WS and press, creating a faced corner.

4 Pin faced corner RS down over the RS of the side panel corner, matching marks. (One way is to stick a single pin through the center of both marks.) Align the seam allowances and slip-stitch or glue-baste them in place. Stitch from the WS of bodice piece, just inside stitching lines on stay fabric. Press bodice allowances open, and the armscye allowances towards the sleeve.

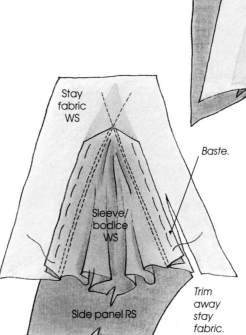

The Long and Short of Flattering Neckline Choices

How to pick appropriate styles for your face shape and neck length

by Jan Larkey

Fluffy scarves tied near the face appear to add pounds to Jan's round face (above). By simply lengthening the scarf (below), she slims perceptibly, without changing outfits.

t he most interesting thing about clothing from my point of view isn't what it looks like, or even how it's made. It's how dramatically clothing can change the way you look, for better or for worse. Neckline choices in the clothing you make or buy, for example, can flatter or detract from the focal point of your figure: your face, and your neck. Let's start with a quick look at the simple visual principles that give clothing such a powerful impact on the way the world sees us, and then see how the principles apply to necklines.

Clothing's graphic impact

The key to clothing's figure-flattering potential isn't fit, fabric, or color. These are each important, but the primary element in any garment's impact on the total figure is its *style lines*. Style lines include the overall silhouette or outline of the gar-

ment; all its seams, edges, openings, and closures (like hems, waistbands, necklines, plackets, zippers, button strips, and pockets); and any prominent patterns or stripes on the fabric. Some garments, of course, have a stronger visual effect than others, because their style lines are more obvious. But in every garment, from the simplest to the most complex, there are certain dominant style lines which give it its shape and graphic impact.

Broad, straight shoulders, for instance, create a strong horizontal outline. Full, nipped-waist skirts form diagonals, pointing towards the waist. Pleats and tucks typically create strong internal vertical lines, while spreading gathers are internal diagonals, diverging towards the spread and converging towards the gathering. These are all powerful visual devices which lead a viewer's eye in specific directions across your garment, and across you when you're wearing that gar-

ment, either exaggerating or deemphasizing the body shapes nearby.

Once you start to see the style lines in your clothing, you can start using them to your advantage in very simple ways. In the large photos above, for example, Jan is wearing a variety of mock collars, to demonstrate neckline style line possibilities. To evaluate the effect of each one, cover each collar half in both photos in turn. For each collar, the style lines include both the neckline shapes (jewel or V-neck) and the outer contours (rounded or pointed). I think you'll agree that either V-necked collar is more flattering to Jan's short neck and round jawline than either jewel neck, and that in both cases, the pointed collar looks better than the rounded one.

The principle at work here is this: *When a style line repeats a nearby body line, it emphasizes it.* To deemphasize any body shape, or to give the impression of a more

flattering shape, wear a *contrasting* style line nearby, one which reinforces the shape you want to suggest. Let's look at some real-clothes examples.

Change accessories instead of outfits

Is there a flattering way for a woman with a short neck or a round chin to wear a high, circular neckline like a jewel neck or a mock turtleneck? Yes, *if* she creates a lengthening, more angular V-line with an accessory. Notice in the smaller photos of Jan on p. 55 how her fluffed up and high-knotted scarf crowds her face and makes her neck all but disappear. By tying the eye-catching scarf to create the flattering V-neck style line we identified for her using the mock collars, Jan instantly creates the illusion of a longer neck and thinner face. In fact, she seems to have lost about five pounds in only five minutes! Incidentally, this tie-shape scarf is also flattering for women with fuller bosoms as it eliminates the volume of a bow or square knot in the bosom area. After folding the scarf on the bias, then into a long, narrow strip, simply tie a loose knot on one side of the scarf, several inches from the end. Slip the other end through the knot, and tighten.

You can apply the same lengthening idea to a too-short (i.e., too-round) necklace by adding a necklace "extender," a length of chain, string, or thin ribbon connected to each end of the clasp, lowering the necklace into a more flattering V or U shape. This shifts the focal point to the necklace, away from the high neckline, creating a new, stronger style line. Notice Jan's collarless jacket at right on p. 55, which she could use to cover up her necklace extension. It's a wonderful choice for a shorter neck, since it creates more space between her neckline and her face than a collared jacket would.

Here are some additional ideas for visually lengthening short necks and thinning round jawlines:
• Wear necklines that open or dip below the collarbone, such as scoop-, U-, and V-necks, lapels, sailor collars, and strapless and sweetheart gowns.
• Choose hairstyles that are off the neck.
• Wear long, thin earrings.
• Avoid short necklaces, high closed collars, cowls, ascots, collar bands, and turtlenecks,
• Don't repeat round shapes close to your face, or wear round earrings.

Making the most of an asset

Jan has used the principles of figure flattery to give the impression of a more ideal body shape (a longer neck and a thinner

Compare Jan (above) and Judith (below). A low, wide neckline works with Jan's short neck, but Judith's long neck looks exposed. By adding a collar and turning it up, Judith softens the effect without losing length.

face) without actually changing her shape at all. But what if you're lucky enough to have the long neck that our culture finds attractive? ("Average" necks are about one hand's width, using your own hand, from collar bone to jaw. Your neck is "long" if the distance is greater than that; "short" if it's less.)

Compare the photos of Jan and Judith on the facing page, both wearing low, wide, and open necklines. Jan's scoop neck works because it suggests plenty of distance between her face and her neckline, while Judith's long neck looks a bit exposed in a similar garment.

By adding an open-necked blouse and turning up the collar in back (lower right photo, facing page), Judith fills in the space between her neckline and hairline, while still reinforcing the elegant vertical shape the V opening suggests. Generally, if you've got an "ideal" body shape, you can wear most style lines. Judith can wear all the round, high-necked shapes that don't work for Jan, but she'll want to be cautious with, or wear softer versions of, all the styles that add length to her longer-than-average neck.

Here are some specific recommendations for extra-long, slender necks and thin faces:
• To make your neck length less obvious, wear high collars such as cowls, turtlenecks, ties, ruffles, and buttoned shirts.
• Soften lengthening necklines with short, close-to-the-neck accessories and high, fluffed scarves.
• Allow your hair length to cover the nape of your neck.
• Wear earrings that make a statement and fill in the space between collar and hairline from the side view.

The neck/back connection

My own neck challenge is my spinal curvature, as you can see in the photo at left below. A low scoop neckline reveals a curve in the neck area, especially with a short or upswept hairstyle. A solution I've found easy to use is to tie my scarf to create volume in back and at one side, like the fluffy style that did not work on Jan in the top right photo on p. 55. Instantly, my neckline problem is concealed.

If you have both a curved neck and a full face, simply create more fullness and softer folds at the back of the scarf arrangement that worked for Jan in the lower right photo, p. 55, adjusting until both your neck and face are flattered. You can keep slippery scarves in place with a tiny roll of tape slipped under the knot and pressed down in position. Just be sure you remove the tape from both gar-

ments when you remove the scarf, so it doesn't leave a gummy residue.

A collarless neckline that's cut high on the back of the neck, like the one I'm wearing in the right-hand photo below, offers very effective concealment of my neck curves. If you're a dressmaker, you can adjust your patterns to conceal precisely what you don't want to reveal, as in this case where the neckline has been raised to be exactly where it needs to be.

Here are some tips for curved, sloping necks or osteoporotic shoulders:
• Overall printed fabrics conceal body curves better than solid colors.
• Patterns that have collars can camouflage the curve.
• For collarless necklines, add volume with scarves. Try using leftover fabric to make a matching scarf for your garment.
• Add shoulder pads to fill in the curve of the shoulder.
• Longer hairstyles may help to fill in the curve. □

Jan Larkey is the author of Flatter Your Figure, *available in bookstores, or by mail from her at Box 8258-T, Pittsburgh, PA 15218. She wrote about shoulders and shoulder pads in* Threads *No. 47, skirt lengths and pleats in* Threads *No. 41, and body proportions in* Threads *No. 31.*

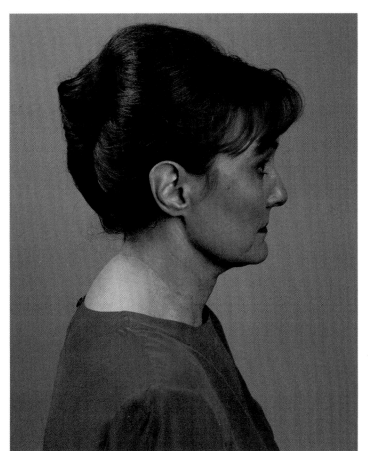 

Jan Larkey's neck is of average length, but complicated by a sloped upper back. A precisely positioned neckline conceals the curve.

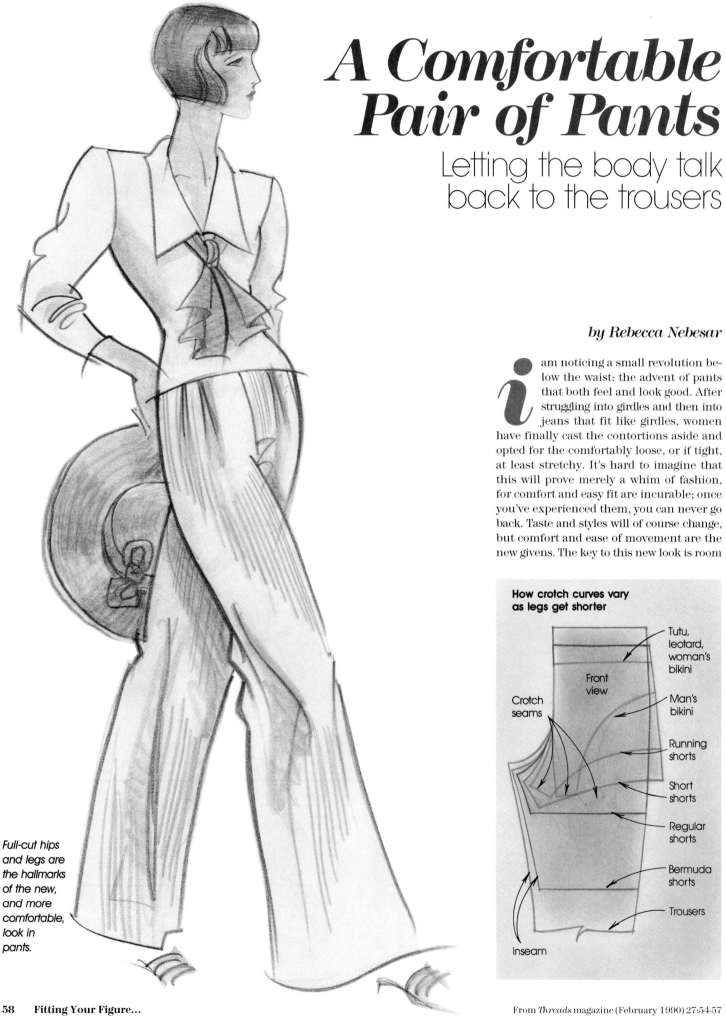

A Comfortable Pair of Pants

Letting the body talk back to the trousers

by Rebecca Nebesar

i am noticing a small revolution below the waist: the advent of pants that both feel and look good. After struggling into girdles and then into jeans that fit like girdles, women have finally cast the contortions aside and opted for the comfortably loose, or if tight, at least stretchy. It's hard to imagine that this will prove merely a whim of fashion, for comfort and easy fit are incurable; once you've experienced them, you can never go back. Taste and styles will of course change, but comfort and ease of movement are the new givens. The key to this new look is room

Full-cut hips and legs are the hallmarks of the new, and more comfortable, look in pants.

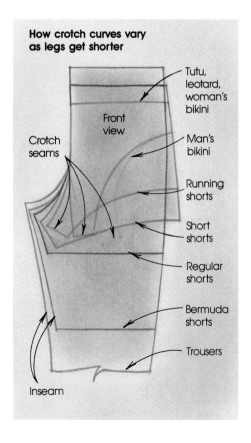

How crotch curves vary as legs get shorter

Tutu, leotard, woman's bikini

Front view

Man's bikini

Crotch seams

Running shorts

Short shorts

Regular shorts

Bermuda shorts

Trousers

Inseam

From *Threads* magazine (February 1990) 27:54-57

to move: fullness in the legs and hips and sometimes a deeper crotch curve.

Fitting oneself into these looser styles is a definite relief from the exertions of the tight old days. Room to move means room to vary. Fit is still important, and all the principles remain the same (for discussions of pants fitting, see *Threads*, No. 17, p. 31; No. 18, p. 32; and No. 26, p. 34). However, when pants are tight, the least disagreement between the shape of the body and the shape of the pants is immediately telegraphed to the surface, and it usually disrupts the fit even in places where it's good, making fitting tricky, mysterious, and subtle. Inherent limitations in the art and design of standard trousers, not women's bodies, account for most pants-fitting problems. You can diet all you want, but there's no way that standard pants will fit both the legs and the crotch perfectly, and the tighter they get, the less they really fit. To see why, let's examine some ways that patterns have evolved to cover our legs and our waists at the same time.

Built for comfort, built for speed

We often think pants show everything, but they don't. Tight pants are a kind of body disguise and restricter, like a girdle. Ordinary trousers are cut like two cylinders, joined at the top, as if to fit an upside-down *V*. But the actual shape of the crotch (from the front) isn't a *V;* it's more like the bottom half of an *H*. Diapers are a great way to fit this shape: a straight piece of fabric

loops effortlessly down the front through the crotch and back up again.

Bathing suits, leotards, and brief-style underpants reinforce the point about our true shapes; these garments don't have legs, so they can simply fit the crotch. I was baffled the first time I looked at a pattern for the bottom section of a tutu—there was no curve in the crotch! I was so used to curved crotch seams that I'd never questioned them. The drawing on the facing page shows what happens to pants patterns as the legs get shorter. Notice that the crotch-seam curve gets straighter, until it straightens out completely, becoming a fold line for the tutu or leotard, which has no legs. The line that starts out as an inseam on the trousers (to fit the upside-down V), becomes a sideways, horizontal crotch seam (to fit the bar of the H) on the leotard. As long as the length of the curve doesn't change, the crotch still fits. The movement of the legs is unrestricted, and the shape of the body is completely revealed, which is why Superman (and dancers and athletes) always wears trunks and tights, instead of trousers.

If fitted legs aren't required, you can cover the legs and the crotch without drawing curves. For example, the Turkish patterns in the drawing below provide both on-grain and bias-pants variations, with waists either gathered or smooth, and echo certain exotic contemporary silhouettes, even though they evolved long before pants developed in the West. In each case, the crotch seams are perfectly straight lines.

When the pattern has no legs, of course we refine the pattern shapes to conform to the body, with less width in the front and more in the back to cover the buttocks. The shape can be further refined with a curved center-back seam so the seam sits a little between the cheeks. Women don't need a center-front seam, but for men it's best to have one that slightly curves away from the center, the *opposite* way from the trouser standard. Elasticized leg openings complete the fit.

The standard trousers

When we add fitted legs back to the pattern, we add new problems, which pattern-makers have solved with some ingenious compromises. It's no longer possible to precisely fit the crotch, nor can the legs spread as easily, but with four seams, and careful shaping at each seam, we can devise a wide variety of fitted effects.

There are several distinct advantages to the way we routinely cut trousers as we do, in four sections, two in front and two in back. The first advantage has to do with a balanced grain. Although it's possible to cut woven trousers in only two pieces, you can't do so and still have the lengthwise grain centered front and back. Having the grain run straight and centered down the middle of the legs both front and back looks crisp, tidy, and not at all comical, and it helps keep the knees from stretching out.

Another advantage is that the side seam is available for fitting the curve of the hip

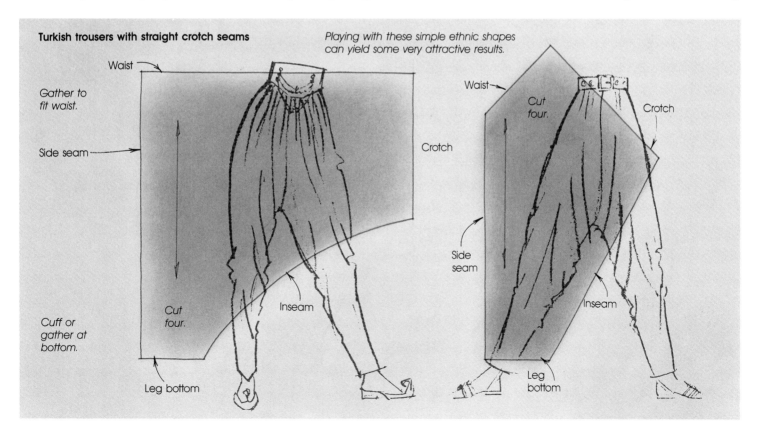

Turkish trousers with straight crotch seams

Playing with these simple ethnic shapes can yield some very attractive results.

Waist

Gather to fit waist.

Side seam

Crotch

Cut four.

Inseam

Cuff or gather at bottom.

Leg bottom

Waist

Cut four.

Crotch

Side seam

Inseam

Leg bottom

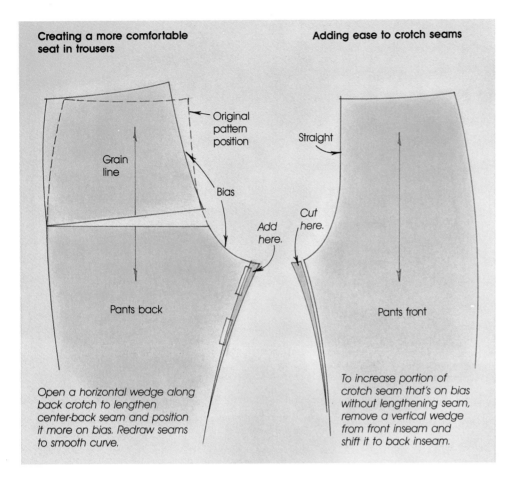

Creating a more comfortable seat in trousers

Original pattern position

Grain line

Bias

Add here.

Pants back

Open a horizontal wedge along back crotch to lengthen center-back seam and position it more on bias. Redraw seams to smooth curve.

Adding ease to crotch seams

Straight

Cut here.

Pants front

To increase portion of crotch seam that's on bias without lengthening seam, remove a vertical wedge from front inseam and shift it to back inseam.

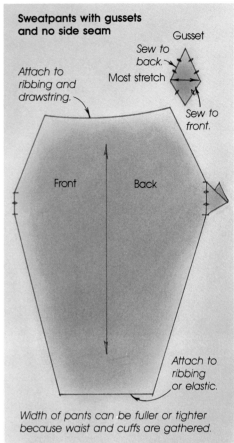

Sweatpants with gussets and no side seam

Gusset

Sew to back.

Most stretch

Sew to front.

Attach to ribbing and drawstring.

Front

Back

Attach to ribbing or elastic.

Width of pants can be fuller or tighter because waist and cuffs are gathered.

and thigh, especially useful in women's pants. Side seams are of course convenient locations for pockets. Furthermore, four-part pants provide an opportunity for great control over the curve of the crotch seams. They allow the designer to carefully position bias areas in the back crotch and seat and to manipulate curves. The inseam, especially at the thigh level, provides flexibility for shaping the pants: cutting tight or full enables the fanny to be either emphasized or concealed. Front and back pieces can be cut separately and differently to match our varied bodily protrusions. Side seams don't have to be mirror images; inseams rarely are. But once they're sewn together and the pants are worn, the seams can look balanced and attractive. A final reason is economics: Four pieces can be laid out without much fabric waste.

But problems arise as soon as we move. When we sit, our seat measurement increases by about 2 in. or more, our lap collapses, our knees push out and require extra fabric, and our rear end pulls on the back of the pants, upsetting all the standing-up fitting. On tight pants the fabric will be strained and rippled. It will wear out at pressure points (knees and seat) and will even sag. Loosely fit pants shift up, down, and out easily with less strain. The fabric shows less wear and lasts longer, but the pants ride up more at the ankles and wrinkle

more in the lap. Which fit better? It's a subjective question, but I know where I stand.

The crotch is the crux

When pants are sewn, the shape of the crotch should resemble the body's lengthwise cross-section, but there's room for lots of subtle adjustments. For men, the decision must be made to shape the trousers to one or the other side of the genitals or to clear a deep enough curve so the center-front seam can be exactly centered. For the latter approach, the pants are cut with the center front on a slight bias and with a longer curve into the inseam. For women, the center front is almost always on grain, and the front crotch curve is shorter.

The cut for the back is similar for men's and women's pants, but women's pants are generally cut with less consideration for movement and sitting. Hence, the center-back seam isn't as much on the bias as it is on men's pants; the reason is more style than anatomy. The more active the pants must be, the more the center-back seam needs to be on a bias.

This trick is accomplished by a maneuver in the patterning of the pants back. A slash is made along the hipline, and the pattern is spread apart in a wedge, tapering to a point at the side seam (drawing at left, above). This is also how a pattern is manipulated for a person with fuller-than-average

buttocks. It causes the upper-back side seam to thrust out, sets the seat area more on the bias, and drops the crease on the straight grain of the leg closer to the center-back seam. The same trick is used in the front, but to a lesser degree. Even for women, the center front can be cut on a slight bias. The important thing to visualize is that the pattern is designed to fit a body with legs spread apart.

Pants designed mainly for sitting in—e.g., riding pants—have been widened, and the crotch curve has been substantially lengthened in just this way. This creates a kind of pocket for the seat, and it also looks dreadful when the wearer stands. I've often thought that the baggy thighs on jodhpurs (real ones, not fashion-cut) were designed as much to draw attention away from the baggy seat as to create freedom of movement. An old tailor described to me how train conductors' pants were once cut just the opposite way—with the center-back seam shortened—because conductors didn't sit much.

For both comfort and good looks, nothing I've seen or worn beats the current fashion of fullness at the hips, controlled at the waist, or at an upper hip yoke, by tucks, pleats, or gathers. The crotch can even be cut with little or no clearance below the body (short in front and in back), as long as the extra fabric is there in the hips to allow for the pull of the seat.

You can also somewhat increase the ease of the center-back seat area without changing its length by shifting the inseam to the front an inch or so at the pattern-adjusting stage (drawing at left, facing page). This increases the amount of the seam on the bias and thus provides more give for movement.

It's important to locate the center-back seam so that it sits gently and slightly between the cheeks and doesn't sag under the seat, flatten it, or have extra lengthwise folds. The curve should begin just below the tail bone. If the fabric doesn't recover well from stretching, the center-back seam should be reinforced to prevent overstretching and sagging. Usually the most comfortable and attractive position for all the seams to come together is about 1 in. to 1½ in. below the body.

Introducing the gusset

Even the best-fit trousers can't match the comfort of sweatpants. The fabric has some give, and the inside is soft, but the cut also has a lot to do with it. The waist is adjustable, and the crotch is as seamless and giving as that of any pants with legs can be. The crotch is usually gusseted (drawing at right, facing page). In fact, just as a gusset can be added to the underarm curve of a sleeve to increase movement and reduce strain, a gusset can be added to regular trousers, with excellent results. (See "Adding a gusset to a pants pattern" at right.) It's surprising that there aren't more pants with gussets. A gusset increases the inseam length without subtracting from, or adding to, the crotch length.

Men's boxer shorts, and some pajamas, are comfortable, if not elegant, because they lack a center-back seam—it has been replaced with a kind of gusset that extends to the waistline in back. The gusset provides ample room when the wearer is sitting, and it allows the garment to be made in striped material without any chevron effect at center back. Currently available patterns for contemporary pants with gussets are rare; Kwik-Sew's 1415 (men's pajamas and shorts) is the only one I've found.

Gusseted pants may represent the best compromise yet between fitting the crotch and fitting the legs. In the early stages of my pregnancy, sweatpants were just the thing for me. Knit fabric, elasticized waist, gusseted crotch—ah! The ultimate in comfort. On a recent hiking tour of a mountainous region, I happily wore a pair of gusseted khakis that climbed all day and still looked reasonably dressy. With options like these, there's no reason to ever be uncomfortable in a pair of pants. □

Rebecca Nebesar is a frequent contributor to Threads.

Adding a gusset to a pants pattern

by Rebecca Nebesar

To design a gusset into a pair of standard pants, first redraw the area on the pattern that fits the upper thigh and crotch. Lay out the front and back pattern pieces, and line up a straightedge along the center-front seam, starting at the waist. At the point where the crotch curve begins to bend away from the straightedge, make a dot, and label it point A. Do the same on the center-back seam, and label that point B. These dots mark the *break points* of the crotch; i.e, the points where the seams begin to fit the crotch instead of the torso. It is here, from front to back between the legs, that the gusset will go.

With a measuring tape on its edge, measure the front crotch seam from the break point to the inseam along the curve. Then let the tape straighten out within the pattern, mark the new end point, and call it point C. Draw a line from the break point to the new point, and label it A. To adjust the inseam to this new crotch curve, draw a second line from the new point about 5 in. down to the inseam, blending it into the curve (drawing of front, below).

Align the back pattern's inseam with the front inseam, matching the upper notches, and mark the spot where point C hits the back inseam. Draw a line from the back break point to this new point on the inseam, blending it into the inseam, and label it B. Allow an appropriate seam allowance, and cut the patterns along the lines you've drawn: A, B, and the reshaped front inseam.

To draft the gusset itself, draw a cross on a piece of 8½-in. by 11-in. paper so that each line is centered on the page. You can make your gusset whatever width you want, but 4 in. is a good place to start. From the center of the cross, measure out 2 in. along the horizontal line. Make a dot and label it point C. Measure line A on the front pattern. With a ruler, draw a line from point C up the vertical leg of the cross the length of line A. Now measure line B; draw a line down from point C to the vertical leg of the cross the length of line B (drawing of back, below). Fold the paper along the vertical leg of the cross, and using the same seam allowance, cut along the new lines A and B. This kite shape is your gusset pattern. Position it on your fabric so that the short cross line follows the line of greatest stretch on your fabric, either the true bias for a woven or across the ribs of a knit.

To sew in the gusset, sew the pants along the side seams and the new inseams so that you have two tubes. Then attach the gusset to one tube so that line B on the gusset matches line B on the pants; do the same with lines A. Then attach the other tube from the waist down the center front along the free sides of the gusset and up to the back waist. —R.N.

Adding a simple gusset to a standard pants pattern

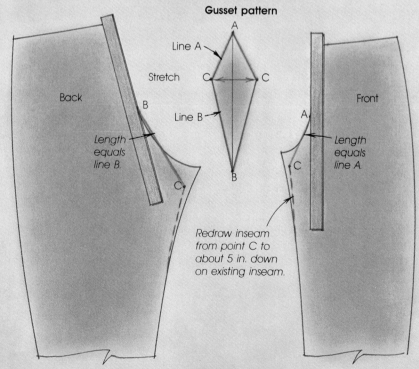

Gusset pattern

Back

Stretch

Front

Line A

A

C — C

Line B

B

Length equals line B.

C

Length equals line A.

A

C

Redraw inseam from point C to about 5 in. down on existing inseam.

Pants for a flat seat

I am a professional dressmaker, but I still can't get a pair of pants to fit me properly. I have a flat seat and am thin and without a lot of curves. The front of pants looks great and the side seams are straight, but there is always too much fabric below the seat in the back.

—Carol A. White,
San Bruno, CA

Joyce Gale replies:
Adjustments to pants should be made by a second person, who can see the pants on you and can rip and fit while you're wearing them.

I assume that you're working with a slacks style (one that hangs straight down from the buttocks), as opposed to jeans. Excess fabric below the seat is caused mainly by a back crotch measurement that is too long for your measurements and a back crotch curve that is too deep. These two causes work hand in hand—the deeper the crotch curve, the longer the crotch length—but they must be corrected separately.

Construct the pants in muslin or, better yet, an inexpensive fabric similar to the fabric that you'll be using. Have your helper pin a dart horizontally across your upper hip, taking in as much as is necessary at the center back, and tapering to nothing at the side seam, to make the pants hang straight down from the point where your buttocks curve out the most. Fold this amount out of the pattern, as shown in step 1 of the drawing below, thereby shortening the back crotch length.

You may still have excess width across the seat, a result of too deep a crotch curve for your particular body shape. Have your helper pin out the fullness in the pants with a long vertical dart. Mark the dart on the pattern. Then transfer the dart to the crotch and inner leg seams so that the amount of fabric removed from these seams corresponds approximately to the amount pinned in

the dart, as shown in step 2 at left. (Note that you can make this adjustment to purchased slacks as well.) Do not lower the crotch in the area indicated or the front and back inseams will not match. The adjustment already made to the back inseam may cause it to be slightly shorter than the front inseam. If so, stretch the back between knee and crotch when you sew. Cut out the revised pattern in fabric, try on the pants again, and make any further adjustments.

Once you've achieved the right fit in one fabric, you'll need to compensate for different weight fabrics or stretchier fabrics. And, your pattern adjustments will be different for each basic pants style (tight jeans, slacks, baggy pants).

Margaret Komives suggests:
First remove the fullness created by the angled center-back seam and the darts. Cut the center-back seam more on grain (as shown in step 1 of the drawing above). Make

the darts smaller, and if there are four darts, perhaps change them to two (step 2). A long, sweeping inseam also creates fullness, so take the elongated point off the inseam (step 3).

If the crotch curve is shallow (the pants have horizontal wrinkles under the seat), lower the crotch curve (step 4)—fullness cannot be removed from the back if the crotch curve is too high. Then see if you can take in the center-back seam at the waistline. Finally, take in the back at the side seams (step 5). Every one of these alterations, including taking in the side seam, can be done without changing the pants front.(*Editors' note:* For more on pants-fitting alterations, see *Threads* No. 18, pp. 32-37.)

About the Fitting *people: Joyce Gale teaches patternmaking and fitting at the L.A. Trade-Technical College. Margaret Komives teaches clothing construction at the Milwaukee Area Technical College.*

Another way to adjust for a flat seat

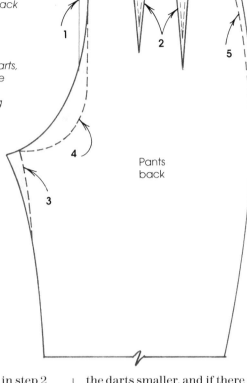

1. *A sloped center back acts as a dart; adjust CB so it's on grain.*

2. *The deeper the darts, the more slope the fanny area has; decrease shaping by making darts smaller.*

3. *Crotch is too deep; move crotch curve inward at inseam.*

4. *Take in CB on grain. Redraw crotch curve to meet CB.*

5. *Take in side seam as needed.*

Pants back

Adjusting pants for a flat seat

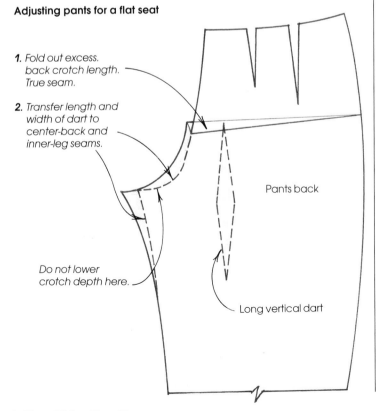

1. *Fold out excess back crotch length. True seam.*

2. *Transfer length and width of dart to center-back and inner-leg seams.*

Do not lower crotch depth here.

Pants back

Long vertical dart

Figure-Flattering Skirts

The right pleats and hemlines complement your proportions

by Jan Larkey

as I travel around the country in my work as a figure and style expert, the single most common question I hear from women is "What kind of clothes should I wear to conceal my tummy curves?" And among the fashion questions they most want answered is "What hemline length is best for me?" I can show you how to solve both puzzles easily in a purely visual way, without measurements, by making some informed decisions about the skirts that you choose to make and wear.

Take a look at the two rectangles at right; which one is thinner? Most people

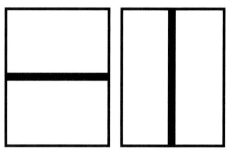

Which rectangle is thinner?

choose the one on the right, but the fact is that the two rectangles are identical. The one on the right simply looks narrower because vertical lines direct your eyes up

and down, while horizontal lines draw your eyes from side to side.

Within every garment's overall shape or silhouette are similar, obvious style lines, created by seams, pleats, creases, pockets, rows of buttons, lapels, and all waistlines and hemlines. These lines can each be categorized as either horizontal or vertical, diagonal or curved. In every case, the interesting fact is that perceived body dimensions are affected by the directions of the style lines.

The simplest rule for applying this fact to our clothing in a flattering way is to wear horizontal lines on the parts of our bodies that we want to appear wider or

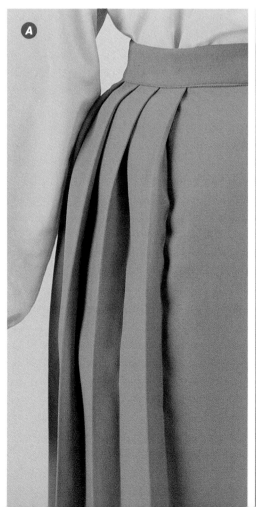

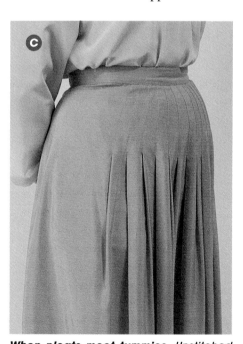

When pleats meet tummies—*Unstitched pleats (photo **A**, at left) increase the impression of width or fullness, while pleats that are stitched down from the waist to the widest part of the abdomen (photo **B**) reduce it. If the pleats are stitched down to lower than the fullest part of the abdomen (photo **C**, above), they emphasize the protrusion by cupping in under the curve.*

A snug-fitting waistband (above) draws attention to the tummy and waist. **A looser band** (below) camouflages the tummy without being obviously loose.

shorter, and wear vertical lines on the body parts that we want to appear narrower or longer.

I've asked a couple of friends to help me demonstrate how we can use the obvious vertical lines of carefully chosen pleats to visually flatten our tummies, and how by thoughtfully positioning the strong horizontal of the hemline we can strengthen or weaken our apparent proportions. That's the secret of the savvy dresser: very few people have ideal figures or proportions, but anyone can dress to appear as if she does.

Tummy-flattening pleats

Most women who feel that they are too curvy in the abdomen or hip simply won't wear pleats. True, a pleat spreading or straining over a curve makes the body appear to be spreading, as well. But correctly handled, pleats can very effectively camouflage curves and will visually narrow unwanted width. The secret is to make sure that the strong vertical lines created by pleats remain straight lines, emphasizing narrowness, and don't become curves, accentuating fullness. Pleats sewn down from the waistline only as far as the fullest part of the abdominal curve, as in photo B on p. 63, will be flattering because from there they will hang straight down.

It's important not to go too far. Pleats stitched down below the level of the fullest part of the curve can create havoc. The stitching tends to curve back under the fullness, emphasizing it, and the pleats won't hang as straight, as you can see in the photo C on p. 63.

If your waist is considerably smaller than your tummy or hips, resist the temptation to fit your waistline. Take a look at the full-length photos of Ann at left, one with her waist fitted snugly, and the other fitted with ease. The snug waist clamors for attention, nearly becoming the dominant line in the outfit, chopping it in half and adding lines of strain to both the skirt and the blouse. The loosely fit waist settles into the background, allows the skirt to hang more smoothly, and minimizes the contour from waist to hip, actually creating the illusion of a flatter tummy. With the waist in the background, the overall shape of the outfit remains a long, narrow rectangle, which of course is much more slimming than the bursting hourglass shape of the fitted waist example.

Finally, remember that the narrower the space between the pleats, the more the impression of narrowness will be reinforced. A few widely spaced pleats, or a few pleats on either side of a wide, flat panel at center front, are not as effective as evenly distributed, narrow pleats, even if only across the front of the skirt or dress.

Leg-flattering lengths

Fortunately for all of us, fashion designers these days seem unable to decide on a hemline length. If we're willing to take a few minutes in front of a full-length mirror with a length of solid-colored fabric, as Judy did with me recently (photos on the facing page), we can determine our own most flattering hemlines.

The length of our skirts, the height of our shoe heels, and our overall height all work together for a single effect, so always test skirt lengths wearing the heel heights you typically prefer. As you can see in the photos, some lengths don't work until you slip into the appropriate shoes.

Judy conducted her test by simply unrolling a folded piece of dark fabric to a variety of hemline positions, while holding it at her waistline. She wore a contrasting but simple top, hose, and her regular shoes, with another favorite pair nearby. This way it was completely apparent what effect the skirt alone had on the outfit, because it didn't blend into any of the other garments.

The critical questions to ask as the skirt lengths roll down are, how does this length work with my total height? And what does this length do for the shape of my legs? With the first question you're looking for pleasing proportions into which to divide your whole figure. This is when you'll notice that higher heels are needed to make longer skirts work. Notice in the photos that with the inappropriate hemlines, Judy's figure looks misproportioned, but with hemlines that work, she looks pleasingly balanced.

When considering your legs, notice that the position of the hemline will change their apparent shape. Usually you'll want to find, as Judy did, a point just above the widest part of your calves, so that a little of the curve above the calf is visible. This is a good hemline for many people, with a variety of heel heights. It's usually good proportionately, and it shows the legs getting narrower. Cutting off the legs at the widest part of the calves is a mistake, unless you want to increase the apparent size of thin legs. There's usually another good level just below that point, but it may require higher heels, as it does for Judy. □

Jan Larkey's book "Flatter Your Figure" is available in bookstores or from her at 126 Hawthorne St., Pittsburgh, PA 15218. She wrote more about solving figure problems in Threads *No. 34, pp. 44-47.*

1.

2.

3.

7.

4.

5.

6.

The mirror test for skirt length—Judy holds a length of plain cloth in front of a full-length mirror to find the ideal hemline. **1.** This length is way too revealing, and divides her unappealingly into thirds. **2.** Still too short; she looks cut in half, and a bit stubby. **3.** Perfect! The proportions are good, and you can see a little of the curve of her calves, so her legs look shapely. **4.** Not so good; the hemline cuts across her calves as they're getting wider, making them look heavy. However, this could be an advantage for thin legs. **5.** Too long; she's starting to look stubby again, but high heels, **6.**, make it work. **7.** Judy's ideal hem length works even better when she adds colored hose and eliminates a waistline to remove every bit of horizontal emphasis, especially once she widens her shoulders slightly and brings attention upward towards her face with a scarf.

Judith King's dress form project starts out with a posterboard and duct tape shell, cut from a formfitting basic pattern.

A Fitting Companion
The simplest custom dress form yet

by Judith King

there's no better way for the seamstress working alone to solve the problem of fit than to use a dress form that duplicates her shape exactly. I've developed a way to make a very serviceable form from inexpensive and easy-to-find materials, as shown above; there's a complete materials list on the facing page.

When it's complete, you can pin into the form and even press or steam garments on it lightly. You can make it over

a weekend without any assistance except for the initial fitting. As long as you've got a well-fitted basic bodice and skirt pattern, or can make one (see "Draping a basic pattern" on p. 69), the process is simple, It works well for all shapes and sizes, even for very asymmetrical bodies, and you can easily use it to make customized half-scale and quarter-scale forms as well. There's a simple method for rescaling patterns in *Basics, Threads* No. 37.

Start with a skintight basic

It's crucial to the success of your form that your basic pattern fit tightly to your figure. Make a test garment from your basic pattern and have a friend pin fit it on your body until it fits like a second skin. Make your adjustments in the order described in the draping sidebar on p. 69. Use a medium-weight nonwoven, like Pellon, instead of muslin; it's transparent and won't pull out of shape. It's easiest to work on a figure that's wearing a leotard or bathing suit, because you can pin into the suit. Just be sure that the garment isn't so tight it constricts or distorts the shape of your body.

You'll need to reshape the front-waist darts as shown in the photo at left to make the bust shape more accurate, and you'll probably have to pinch out some additional darts in unusual places to get the Pellon pattern to conform exactly to your body. For example, a very rounded back will require darts in the back armscye or neckline, and a front chest hollow may require either horizontal or vertical double-ended darts, like those in the lower photo on the facing page, to contour the pattern, and thus the posterboard shell, correctly.

If you are fitting a large, full bust, split the front-waist dart on each side into two darts placed equidistant from the bust point. This will ensure a more rounded, less pointed bust. If the back is very rounded, you may need two darts per side there as well.

Making the posterboard shell

First, make tracings of your adjusted basic pattern, and trim off all the seam allowances, including those at darts. Store the original; you can refer to it in the future if your figure changes. You'll use the traced pattern in all the steps below.

Cutting the posterboard—The posterboard and foam layers should have side seam openings only, none at center front (CF) and center back (CB), so tape the halves of the tracings together if your pattern has center-front or -back seams. Lay the tracings out on the posterboard, and trace the front and back patterns, starting the skirt about 3 in. to 4 in. above knee level. Be sure to mark bust and hip levels on the tracings, along with CF and CB lines and both bust points.

To make the tracings smaller to allow for the thickness of the foam layer, measure ¾ in. in from the bodice and skirt side seams, front and back, and mark new seamlines. At the front and back shoulder, measure ½ in. down from the original line and draw new lines. Extend

From *Threads* magazine (October 1991) 37:48-51

the new shoulder line at the armscye edge so it's the same length as the original line, and blend the upper part of the armscye to meet the end of the new line.

Cut out the posterboard pieces carefully on the new lines. About 2 in. from the waist on the bodice and skirt side seams, taper your cutting line inward so that you are taking off about another ¼ in. at each side seam (total 1 in.) to allow for the buildup of tape that will occur there.

Shaping the bust—At the bodice front, tape the side bust darts first. Tape at right angles to the dart line, then cover the entire dart with tape on both inside and outside. Push gently inward at the diaphragm level under the bust to bring the lower ends of the shaped waist darts together. Tape securely, then tape the curved under-bust portion of the dart.

To give the bust a more realistic shape, measure down from the neck to the approximate point where the valley between the breasts starts, and mark it on the CF line, then slash from this point almost to each bust point and down the CF to the diaphragm level. If the whole chest is concave, start the slash higher, but don't cut through the neckline.

Gently push in the slashed area, making an opening along the CF and creating separate bust shaping, as in the photo on p. 68. This isn't an area of precise fit; just make it look reasonable. Tape the slashed sections securely to the upper portion of the bodice on both the outside and inside of the shell. Join the front and back bodice sections together at the shoulders, taping as you did for the darts, then close one side seam.

Forming the skirt and support disks—At this point, your stand should be prepared and ready to use, as described in the materials sidebar. The following directions will assume you're using something like my dowel-in-a-Christmas-tree-stand idea, with a shoulder-height cross support for the bodice.

Tape the skirt darts closed, then tape the front and back skirt sections together at the side seams. Gently squeeze the skirt cylinder into a rounded shape so the side seams aren't angular.

Place the cylinder on a large piece of paper and, reaching down inside, trace around the inner edge of the lower skirt opening; crossmark on the outside at CF, CB, and the side seams. Draw a straight line from CF to CB and from side seam point to side seam point. Where the two lines cross, draw a circle slightly less than the diameter of your stand rod.

Cut out this pattern and use it to mark

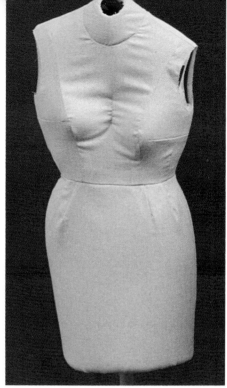

No matter how asymmetrical your figure, the posterboard shell can duplicate it. The shell is covered with thin foam rubber, then with cotton drill, so it's easy to pin into. It's also easy to rescale the pattern to make a custom half-scale form.

To make the form, a fitted basic pattern must be carefully reworked to follow every body contour, using whatever additional dart shapes are appropriate, like the upper bust darts shown below.

one of the pieces of thick pillow foam. Cut the foam with a knife, or by squeezing tightly and cutting with scissors. Label CF, and cut out the center circle. Matching the CF marks on the spacer and the shell, fit the spacer into the lower end of the skirt cylinder, as in the cutaway drawing on p. 68, and secure by taping across the bottom.

Temporarily tape the second bodice side seam together, then trace around the outside of the shell at the waistline

edge; this tracing will probably be more hexagonal than oval. Mark the tracing just as for the skirt, and draw in the lines and center circle. Cut another piece of the pillow foam to this pattern. Reopen the bodice side seam that you temporarily closed, and attach the stand, as shown in the illustration.

Before making the foam and cloth covers, you'll need to add a neck shape to the posterboard shell. The drawing on p. 68 gives complete instructions. ⇨

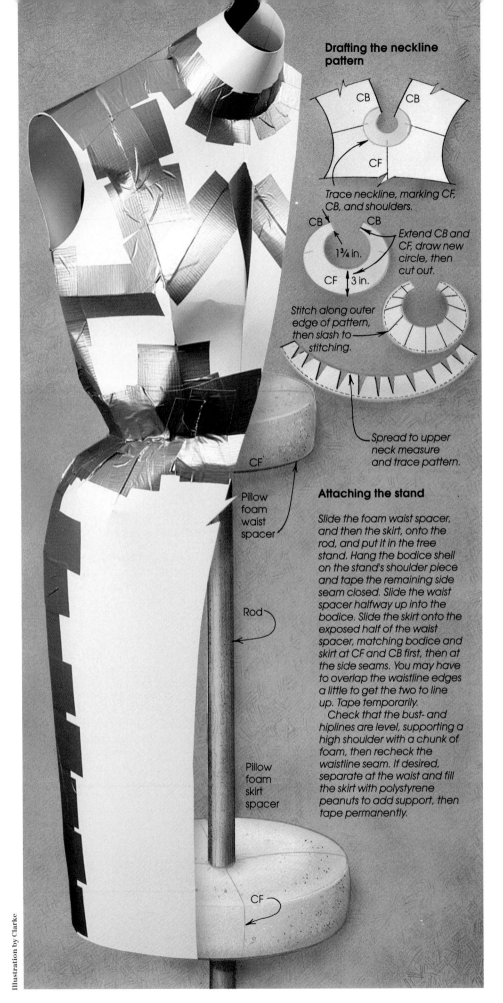

Drafting the neckline pattern

CB CB

CF

Trace neckline, marking CF, CB, and shoulders.

CB CB

1¾ in.

Extend CB and CF, draw new circle, then cut out.

CF 3 in.

Stitch along outer edge of pattern, then slash to stitching.

Spread to upper neck measure and trace pattern.

CF

Pillow foam waist spacer

Rod

Pillow foam skirt spacer

CF

Attaching the stand

Slide the foam waist spacer, and then the skirt, onto the rod, and put it in the tree stand. Hang the bodice shell on the stand's shoulder piece and tape the remaining side seam closed. Slide the waist spacer halfway up into the bodice. Slide the skirt onto the exposed half of the waist spacer, matching bodice and skirt at CF and CB first, then at the side seams. You may have to overlap the waistline edges a little to get the two to line up. Tape temporarily.

Check that the bust- and hiplines are level, supporting a high shoulder with a chunk of foam, then recheck the waistline seam. If desired, separate at the waist and fill the skirt with polystyrene peanuts to add support, then tape permanently.

Completing the posterboard layer: To shape the bust more realistically, the CF of the shell was slashed, then spread and taped. Then the bodice and skirt sections were hung on the completed stand. Foam spacers at waist and hem hold the form to the stand and help keep its shape.

Making the foam layer

Because the foam can stretch and mold itself to the posterboard, I usually eliminate the waistline seam on this layer; it makes the form smoother. Trace off new full-length front and back patterns after joining the original bodice and skirt tracings. At the side seams, the tracings may overlap or spread apart a little. An overlap of up to ⅝ in. won't matter, but if the difference is more than that, you're better off with separate bodice and skirt parts, as in the photo on the facing page.

Move the skirt darts so they're in line with the bodice darts where possible. If you have to make the skirt dart smaller to fit the bodice dart, take the difference off at the skirt's side seam.

Lay the new patterns, and the old neck piece, on the foam sheeting and trace them using a marking pen. Cut along the marked line (no seam allowances) with sharp scissors. Cut out all darts, too.

Glue the darts closed first, using contact cement. Work with one dart at a time, applying glue to each leg of the dart with a small paintbrush. Let the cement dry a minute and then press the dart edges together. Let dry for a few more minutes before proceeding to the next dart; I work on one foam piece while another is drying. Once all darts have been glued, glue the shoulder seams together and let dry. Glue one long side seam and let the whole thing dry.

Place the foam cover on the form and smooth into place, then glue the remaining side seam, as I'm doing in the photo on the facing page. The foam should fit snugly against the form, so trim away any excess at the side seam if necessary. If you have to trim more than about ¾ in. from the front and back, cut apart the first side seam as well, so you can trim both sides equally.

Fit the neckpiece after the body fits well, trimming away at CB if necessary before gluing. Glue the CB seam, then lift the neckpiece off to apply glue to the neckline and neckpiece.

The fabric cover

The cotton drill layer is one piece, with a zipper from neckline to below the elasticized hem. Working with the original tracings, mark the wrong side of the drillcloth by tracing around the face-

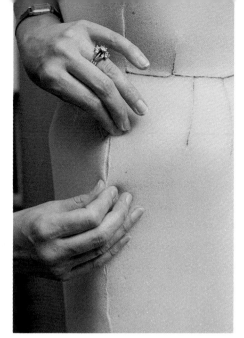

The foam rubber layer, cut from the refitted basic pattern, is assembled with contact cement applied to the edges and pressed together. All that remains is to put on a cotton drill cover, and the form is ready to use.

down pattern pieces; include the waistline seams. As you lay the pieces out, leave enough room between them to allow for 1-in. seam allowances all around and add a CB opening with seam allowances for a zipper. At the skirt hem, add about 4 in. to 5 in. Mark the right and left halves of all the pieces (check this step twice, especially if there are significant differences between sides), then add the 1-in. seam allowances. Trace the neck-piece, but add a 2½-in. seam allowance at the upper-neck edge, for finishing.

Constructing the cover—After cutting the fabric pieces, staystitch the neckline, armscye, and waistline curves, then stitch and press all darts. For the shaped front-waist darts, start at the waistline edge, stitch up to the diaphragm level, then pivot to stitch the curved portion to the tip of the dart. Clip the seam allowance at the corner, and reinforce the stitching there.

Stitch and press CF and side seams on the bodice and skirt, then stitch and press the shoulder seams. Join the bodice and skirt units at the waist, pressing the waistline seam up. For reinforcement, add a row of topstitching on the bodice about $\frac{1}{16}$ in. from the seam. I stitch bust- and hip-level lines with a contrasting thread at this point. You can hand baste the lines on the finished form with embroidery thread if you prefer. Clip the bodice neckline seam allowance and attach the fabric neckpiece.

Cut 1½-in.-wide bias strips from the

drillcloth to finish the armscye. Trim the armscye seam allowance to within $\frac{1}{16}$ in. of the staystitching, and begin the stitching in the underarm area, matching one edge of the tape to the cut edge of the armscye. Turn the tape end under about $\frac{1}{4}$ in. as you start applying it so you have a finished end when the taping is completed; allow the other end to overlap the folded end by about $\frac{3}{4}$ in. Fold the tape over the armscye edge, smooth and pin it, then stitch it in the ditch of the seam.

At the hem of the skirt, turn up about $\frac{3}{4}$ in., press, then topstitch $\frac{1}{2}$ in. to $\frac{5}{8}$ in. from the folded edge and insert a strip of elastic in the resulting casing.

To insert the zipper, press under the CB seams on the seamline, then butt each folded edge up against the teeth of the zipper, leaving them exposed and the excess length hanging below; it'll be tucked out of sight later. Stitch along the zipper, starting and stopping at the line of stitching for the casing at the lower edge of the skirt, and reinforcing the ends by backstitching.

Fitting the cover—First try the cover on yourself to check its accuracy, making corrections if necessary. Gently work the cover onto the form, working from the bottom up rather than pulling the cover down over the form. When you've got the cover on, smooth it over the shoulders and bust and then work down to the waist, smoothing the skirt into place. Try to smooth the seam allowances flat wherever possible.

Keep the CF, CB, and side seams lined up and the bust- and hip-level lines straight on the form. Another pair of hands is helpful for this step, if only to hold the form steady while you work with the cover. Once the cover is in place, zip it closed.

To finish the neckline, clip the upper edge just enough to allow its extra length to be tucked in between the foam and the posterboard along the upper neckline edge. Finish the bottom by pulling the elastic as taut as possible and tying securely. The lower end of the cover will pull in under the lower edge of the form. Tuck the ends of the elastic and the zipper back in under the cover.

To shape the bust at CF, I stitch through the cover and the foam layer with a heavy, doubled thread and tie it to the stand, pulling the thread until the cover conforms to the posterboard. □

Judith King is a Certified Home Economist. She has taught a fitting class for professionals at the School for Needle Arts in Atlanta, GA.

Draping a basic pattern

The first step is to establish reference points on the figure. You need to mark CF and CB lines, neck-, waist-, and hiplines, shoulder and bust points, shoulder lines, and side seams. I prefer the drapee to wear a leotard, so I can mark and pin onto it.

I chalk mark center lines front and back, using a plumb line to make sure the lines are vertical. To find the neckline, I tie a light chain around the neck; regular string is too light, but it works fine for establishing the waist. I mark bust and shoulder points with crossed pins so I can feel the marks through the fabric, and I chalk in the shoulder line. I draw vertical side seams, from the armscye down; sometimes the leotard's side seams are usable guides.

I cut enough Pellon to cover the entire front and draw a line down the center, which I pin to the CF line on the figure. Then I smooth and pin the fabric over the body, trimming off excess as I go and making sure there are no wrinkles or tension lines in the drape. I work up to the neckline, then out to each shoulder, then down the armscyes to the bust, completing both sides at each level before moving on. At the bust level, I fold out the first (horizontal) dart, removing only enough fabric so that what's left hangs straight down from the bust, to be removed with a vertical waist dart.

I start the back by pinning along the CB line and work up to the neck and down the sides to the waist. The back darts point to the shoulder blades, unless some other point is more prominent. Ideally, the darts will be at the shoulder and waist, and the waist darts will angle out to the blades.

Next I mark the hiplines with masking tape, making sure the line is horizontal, and at the widest point on the figure. I pin the skirt the same way, starting at the centers, but I smooth out to the hips first, and attach front and back at the same time, so I can pin the sides together. Then I smooth up towards the waist, forming darts as needed. When I'm done, I mark along all the seams and darts, and true the lines with the fabric flat to make the final pattern. –J.K.

Padding a Dress Form

Fusible interfacing and cotton batting reshape a form to match your figure

by Suzanne Pierrette Stern

before you can drape a garment for yourself, you must have a mannequin, or dress form, that represents your own body. The classic method, which we practiced in Paris in the late 40s, and which is still in use today in couture sewing, is to pad a commercial dress form to approximate the shape and measurements of the body you'll be sewing and draping for. To make the shape exact, we then drape a muslin fitted shell directly over the padded form (which is much easier than draping directly on the body), then put the muslin on the body and fit it closely. Once the muslin is sewn up, we put this fine-tuned "second skin" back on the form and stuff in more batting, or remove it as needed, to fit the muslin.

In this article, I'll show you how to complete the first step, padding the form to your measurements, as I'm doing in the photo at right, in preparation for draping the muslin. All you need for this first step is a form, some cotton batting, an inexpensive nonwoven fusible interfacing, and a measuring tape. The form can be any sort, as long as it's sturdy, and smaller all around than you are, because obviously you can't make it smaller. It's best to use

Besides being the most sensible method of customizing a dress form for anyone who already has one, this process is a wonderful way to develop a few often-neglected skills essential for successful sewing and fitting, such as a good eye, an understanding of the shapes of the body, and some experience draping fabric to fit it.

From *Threads* magazine (December 1992) 44:35-37

Taking measurements

The couture workroom fitting process starts with accurate measurements. The method we used in Paris is very effective, because it uses a few easy-to-find, fixed points on the figure. These are the first thoracic vertebra (that's the first big bump you feel on your spine as you move your hand down your neck), the bust points, and the waistline, which you mark on yourself with a ribbon or string. Also locate a vertical line, front and back, which separates the body from the arm, along which a fitted armscye would fall. (We'll refine the position of this line at the muslin stage.) Here are the measurements you'll need:

- *Front shoulder width (the French term is* carrure*), taken from one armscye line to the other, across the chest, as high as possible.*
- *Back carrure, again from armscye line to line, but across the back.*
- *Bust circumference.*
- *Waistline circumference.*
- *Hip circumference.*
- *Center-front length, measured from the base of the neck to the waistline, and then to the floor.*
- *Center back, taken from the first thoracic vertebra to the waist, and to the floor. (These last two establish your vertical proportions.)*
- *Bust, measured over the shoulder from the first thoracic vertebra to the bust point and on to the waist in a straight line.*
- *Distance between the bust points. (These last two precisely position the bust points.)*
- *Neck circumference at its base.*
- *Armscye circumference.*

The initial padding and draping are done on only half the figure (traditionally the right side) to save time and effort, so you'll also need to know what half of the horizontal measurements are, measuring from the center-front and -back lines. Measurements are necessary, but the same ones could fit many different shapes; note how the body measurements differ from the form's measurements, but remember that the most important thing is to observe your body in the mirror or in photos to be sure of the actual shape, and how it differs from the form.

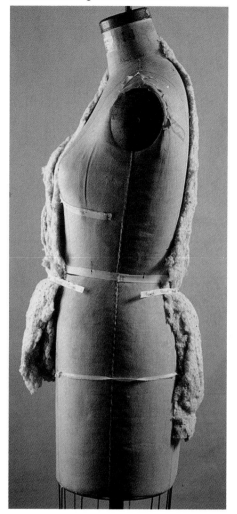

Because you start with a form that's smaller all around than the final results you need, you can reposition bust shapes and points, and the waistline, which was lowered in the example shown here, as well as recontouring the entire form.

the kind of batting you can tear into shape with your hands, instead of needing to cut it, but you can use any kind. I prefer upholstery batting, which I'm using in the photos. Besides measurements (see above), a few good photos of yourself—or the person you're fitting—from the front, back, and side, in a leotard or bathing suit, will be a big help, but you can do it all with just a mirror if necessary.

Padding

On the form in the accompanying photos, I've lengthened the waist and added a lot of extra size all over, especially at buttocks and tummy, as you can see in the side view above. If you're moving the waist, check to see that your form is still smaller than your figure at the new waistline. Since it was smaller to begin with, you should be able to raise or lower it an inch or two.

The padding process consists simply of pressing pieces of batting to the form and molding them to the shape you need. You can start anywhere, either in front or in back, but it's best to work from the top down. Lap over the center-front and -back lines on the form about 2 in. Use pins sparingly to hold the batting in place.

With the picture of yourself firmly in mind, ask yourself at each place on the form "Does my body resemble the form here? Should I add or not?" For example, if your measurements and observation tell you to make the bust a little fuller and slightly lower, place the batting over it and mold the point to a lower position, checking both the measurements and the photos, and yourself in the mirror. At the same time, consider the space over the bust and shoulder. In my example I covered the form all the way to the shoulder to meet the fuller back, and in this case, extended the shoulder width slightly with the help of a little shoulder-pad-shaped triangle of manila paper bent

over the form's shoulder under the batting. You may not have to cover the shoulder at all. The batting's a bit squashy, so it should look a little big, because it will compress slightly under the fusible layer that will hold the batting in place.

Pad the waist as needed, carefully observing whether you need more in front or back. Smooth the side where the front and the back join, then turn your attention to the hips. Does the figure you're making have more tummy, or bigger hips or buttocks, or a little of each? Reproduce whatever is needed, but recheck your waistline position because the hips may need to start higher or lower than on the form.

Pressing on the fusible

When you are satisfied with the looks of your molding, recheck your measurements, adjust if necessary, then put a ribbon or tape of some kind around the waist from center front to center back

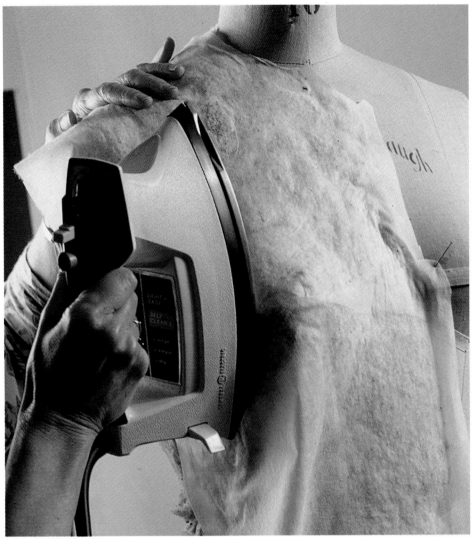

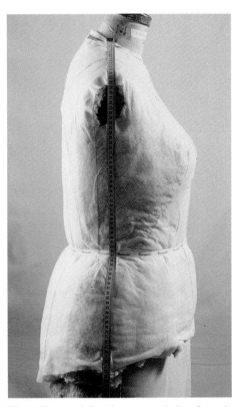

When the padding is covered, the form is marked with lines for the neck, waist, center front and back, side, shoulder, and over the bust. Position the tape measure along the lines you need using measurements and your eye, and use it as a guide for your marker. Mark the waistline with a piece of tape or ribbon.

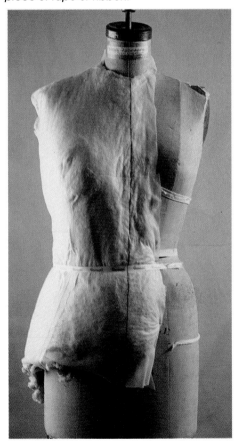

Covering and marking the batting: *To keep the batting in place, press strips of soft, nonwoven fusible interfacing over it. You can snip and slash wherever you need to to get the fusible to conform to the shapes you've molded. To shape under the bust, for instance, cut away the excess, and overlap the cut edges.*

and pin it securely to mark the waistline.

Cut some strips of the thin, soft fusible, about 8 to 10 in. wide and a bit longer than your padding. Starting at center front and overlapping it by a couple of inches, smooth the fusible up to the shoulder and down to the bottom of the hips, tacking it in place with an iron set on medium heat, no steam (don't worry if the instructions call for steam—you won't be washing this interfacing). You will have to cut around the neckline, slash at the bust level, and overlap as necessary at the valley between the bust points. Then press the whole surface down with the iron, as I'm doing in the photo above.

You can slash and overlap the fusible however you please as long as it gives you the shape you need. Cover the whole surface, overlapping the center back as you did for the front. When you're done, put another tape around the waistline on top of the one below the fusible.

Marking

To drape the muslin, you'll need some lines of reference on the fusible as shown in the photos of the finished padding at right. Use a plumb line (any object tied to the end of a string makes a plumb line) to mark the centers. Draw in the neckline, using your waist-to-neck measurements to check its position in front and back. Use these same measurements to check the waistline-to-floor length.

The armscye only needs to be approximate. Just make it smaller than your measurement; you can wait for the fitting to adjust it. Now you're ready to prepare the muslin and to drape it into a torso. See you at the next article.

Suzanne Pierrette Stern wrote about her days working for couturier Jacques Fath in Paris in Threads *No. 40. She currently teaches draping at Los Angeles Trade-Technical College.*

Draping a Cover for a Padded Form

Placing the grain is the key

by Suzanne Pierrette Stern

every sewer has heard about the importance of grain in garment construction and design. Few truly understand it, perhaps because few sewers have had any experience with draping. In this installment of our series on reshaping a dress form, you'll have an opportunity to experience both draping and grain directly. Working with the grain is the basis of the draping process, which we'll use to create the form's cover (In the previous article, I described padding the form.) In future installments we'll perfect the draped muslin cover by fitting it directly on the body.

What you'll need
For the initial draping, you'll need only some pins, a marking pen or chalk, and a torso-length of ordinary 45-in.-wide muslin, since, as with the padding, we'll only be draping half the form. We'll add the other side later. Select a muslin that's neither too tightly woven nor too soft, because you'll be tearing it into usable pieces and pulling a few threads on each piece to establish the grainlines.

After straightening the grain of each piece, for which you'll need a steam iron and an L-shaped ruler, we'll pin the muslin to the padding, shaping it to the form with a vertical seam from shoulder to hip over the bust point. You can see the shape of this seam in the photo on the facing page, in which I've folded the left-hand side of the muslin along the seamline. There will be a similar seam in back over the shoulder blade. These seams are called *princess* seams; they are the easiest way to shape the flat muslin to the contours of a typical figure.

Finally, we'll take the muslin off the form and transfer its outline to paper, creating a pattern from which we'll later make a full-torso muslin. For this step you'll need some large sheets of paper (dotted pattern paper is ideal, but any plain paper will do) and a pin-point tracing wheel, available from suppliers of professional sewing equipment, like Greenberg & Hammer, 24 W. 47th St., New York, NY 10019; (212) 246-2835. You'll also need about a 20- by 36-in. surface you can pin into, like a scrap of bulletin board, or a folded sheet. To neaten the lines on the muslin and pattern, and to make sure they match across the seams, we'll *true* the lines, as described on p. 76.

Preparing the muslin
Estimate how much muslin you need by measuring the form. Start 2 in. above the shoulder seam at the neck, going down to the bottom of the padded torso. I used about 30 in. Tear the muslin to length so you'll have a true crossgrain guideline. Then tear it vertically into four equal pieces, two for the front, two for the back. Don't press the muslin, because the next step is to pull lengthwise and crosswise threads to mark the grain in certain positions (see *Basics, Threads* No. 45); pressing will make this more difficult.

On two of the pieces, pull two adjacent threads 1 to 1½ in. away from a torn edge on the lengthwise grain. These lines will mark center front (CF) and back (CB).

Don't use a selvage edge—it's too hard to square. Position the selvage on the opposite side, where it will be trimmed away later. About 7 to 9 in. from the top of each of these two pieces, pull two threads on the crossgrain. On the two remaining pieces, pull two straight-grain threads in the center of each piece, then pull two crossgrain threads about 10 to 12 in. down. These will be the side-front and -back pieces. I've thread-traced the pulled threads with red in the photos so you can see them; you don't need to do this.

Now each piece needs to be perfectly squared and thoroughly steam-pressed on the ironing board. First press out all ragged edges, so they do not interfere with your view of the grains. Press out all the creases while straightening the grains by eye as much as possible. Then verify with a square ruler that the torn edges at cross- and straight grains are at a perfect right angle, checking, pressing, then rechecking. When you're satisfied, do the same to the remaining pieces. I can't overemphasize just how important this grain-straightening is, because the grain is at the heart of the draping process, as you'll see below; if it isn't perfectly square, your efforts will be frustrated continually.

Draping the form
The main principle of draping is: First place the grains, and then use the excess in seams, darts, or design lines. As I describe below how to drape each of the four pieces of muslin, you'll see what placing the grains means in this project.

Professional dress forms already have seams on their covers running vertically over the bust, and in back over the shoul-

> *The main principle of draping is: First place the grains, and then use the excess in seams, darts, or design lines.*

der blade area (see the dress form in the photo at right). This is because the princess line, which the seam marks, is so commonly used as a guide in draping and fitting processes. Since we're personalizing the dress form by padding it, we have to redraw the princess line on the padding. You can use the same placement as on the dress form, or change the angle of the line slightly if you think that would make it more visually pleasing on your remodeled form, as long as the line still passes over the bust point. Use your tape measure to position the line, draping the tape over the shoulder and bust. Pin the tape in place and mark along its edge onto the padding. Do the same in back, starting from the same point on the shoulder as you did in front.

Placing the center-front piece—Arrange one of the pieces prepared for the centers so that the lengthwise pulled threads are on the form's CF, while the crosswise threads hit the bust point. When these lines are perfectly horizontal and vertical, the grains will have been placed for this piece. There should be about 2 in. of fabric above the shoulder. Pin at the neckline on CF, and 2 or 3 in. below. The fabric should fall straight down, but over the contour of the bust.

From the last pin, smooth the crossgrain across the upper chest, and pin. From that pin smooth the straight grain up to the shoulder and pin. These two movements are drawn directly on the muslin shown in the photo at right. Smoothing with the grain in this fashion avoids bias movements which might stretch the fabric. Never tug or pull the fabric in any direction.

Cut away the corner of muslin at the neck, and clip around the neckline to release all tension. In order not to overcut, place the tip of the open scissors where you need to stop and bend the fabric to the scissors, then clip. Pin at the shoulder and near the neck.

Smooth the muslin over the bust, keeping the straight grain aligned with CF, all the way past the waist to the bottom, and the crossgrain truly parallel to the floor. Pin at the bust point and secure CF all the way down. There will be excess at the CF bust level between the bust points. In the photo, I've taken up the excess in a small temporary dart; you can do this, too, if you like, or just leave it. The dart will not be marked or transferred to the pattern. We'll deal with this excess permanently during the fitting.

Trace the princess line onto the muslin from the line on the padding underneath. Trim away the muslin leaving

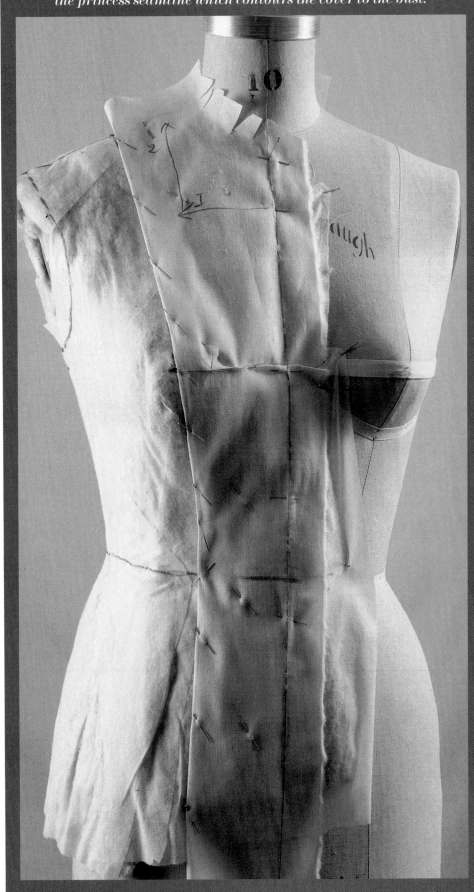

Reshaping a dress form to create a perfect replica of your figure starts with padding, and continues with draping the padding, the initial stage of fitting the muslin cover. The first section to drape is the center front, shown here completed from a perfectly on-grain center front to the princess seamline which contours the cover to the bust.

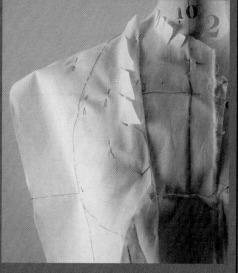

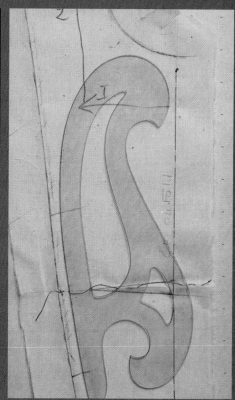

Placing the side grains

To ensure that the grain of the side piece (marked with red thread, left) is perfectly vertical, check it with a plumb line. Once pinned to follow the form's curves, the grainline above the bust level no longer stays straight (above). The edge that goes under the previous piece has been trimmed and clipped to lie flat underneath.

Truing the markings on the muslin into clear, precise lines (shown above) is easy with a French curve.

about a 1½-in. folding allowance, and clip into the allowance a few times so it will lie flat. Then fold along the line, pinning diagonally all the way down, making sure there are no wrinkles. When you're satisfied that everything looks good (the photo on p. 74 was taken at this point), move the pins back an inch or two from the princess line and fold the muslin back to expose the line for draping the side piece over it.

Placing the side piece—Hold one of the pieces with the pulled threads in the center in front of the side front and place the straight grain in perfect vertical alignment, as in photo 1 above. Match the length with the piece already there, and place the first pins on the grain at the bust level (don't worry if the crossgrain pulled threads don't line up with those on the front), then work down to the end. Still working below the bustline area, smooth the fabric toward the side seam, pin, then smooth toward the princess line and pin.

Starting below the armhole, smooth the muslin up toward the shoulder and the princess line. As you can see in photo 2 above, the grain will completely change direction to follow the shape, but that's

all right. Pin where necessary. Trace the side seam and princess line onto the muslin, and trim and then clip along the lines, leaving a generous seam allowance as before.

Fold over the seam of the front piece to bring it back on top of the side piece, on the princess line, matching the two lines as you pin, as in photo 4 on p. 76. Mark the shoulder seams and trim near them, then move the pins back from the shoulder and side seam, freeing those lines for the back pieces.

Placing the back pieces—The pieces for the back go on in the same way as those for the front. Start with the center piece, then overlap that onto the side piece, at the back princess line, checking always that the grains are perfectly horizontal and vertical (see photo 3 on p. 76). The center muslin should initially extend above the shoulder by about 2 in. When you pin along the CB from the neckline to the bottom, make sure it is just smooth, and not too tight.

Finishing up—Check to see that the front and back princess lines match perfectly at the shoulder, then overlap the front pieces onto the back ones along the shoul-

der line. Trim the side seams leaving plenty of excess seam allowance, but don't overlap one allowance over the other. Pin them together as shown in photos 3 and 4 of the completed drape.

Before removing the muslin, you must carefully mark it: Each seamline should be outlined on both sides, and cross marks must be placed at right angles to the seams to show how one side fits against the other, just like notches in a pattern. Mark near the hipline and at the waistline, and put two cross marks above the waist on the princess lines and one at the side seam, as in photos 3 and 4.

Both the neckline and armscye must be drawn freehand. In each case, make the openings smaller than you think that you'll need. The neckline should follow the dress form's neck in back, then dip down about ½ in. below it at center front. The armscye likewise should only drop about ½ in. below the metal plate on the form, or whatever device your form has for indicating the armhole. If there's no such device, just make the opening quite small, and correct it at the fitting stage. Look over everything, compare the shape with the two photos on the facing page, and when you're satisfied, remove the muslin piece by piece.

Making the pattern

To prepare the muslin for copying, flatten it (don't press!) and true up all the lines with a straightedge and a French curve. I use a No. 20 French curve, available in art supply stores; it's shown in the right-hand photo on p. 75.

Truing—The purpose of truing is simply to turn sketchy lines into clear, precise ones, and also to check that the various pattern pieces fit together exactly. Use the French curve and straightedge to re-draw each marked line, keeping all the subtlety of the curves. Smooth out only the obvious wobblings of your initial marks. Shift and flip the French curve in any way necessary to follow the curves that you want to draw, moving along a line in sections until you have one smooth curve. At the meeting of two curves at a seamline, such as at the underarm or neckline, the curves should hit the seam so that they meet each other in a perfectly straight line, if only for a short distance. Put the pieces side by side to check this.

Measure each line carefully to confirm that it matches the line it will be stitched to, and confirm each cross mark. These will be helpful in sorting out which line is too short if you encounter any errors.

Transferring to paper—Draw a straight grainline on your paper, then, with a square ruler, draw the crossgrain in approximately the same positions as on the muslin. With the paper on your pinnable surface, place the center front of the muslin piece on the line representing the straight grain with the bust-level cross-grain matching its own line. Place a push pin where they meet. Line up the center front up and down, then line up the crossgrain, holding both in place with push pins. From these points, smooth out the muslin in all directions keeping the grains squared, and pin. When all is secured, use the tracing wheel to go over every line and cross mark.

After transferring each piece to paper, take off the muslin and true all the pin-marked lines with the rulers as you trace them in pencil. The center-front piece is generally cut in one piece, so mark the center-front line "CF on fold." Then you can add generous seam allowances all around. You're ready now to cut the pattern out and try it on the figure. □

Suzanne Pierrette Stern wrote about her experiences working for couturier Jacques Fath in Paris in Threads No. 40. *She currently teaches at Los Angeles Trade-Technical College.*

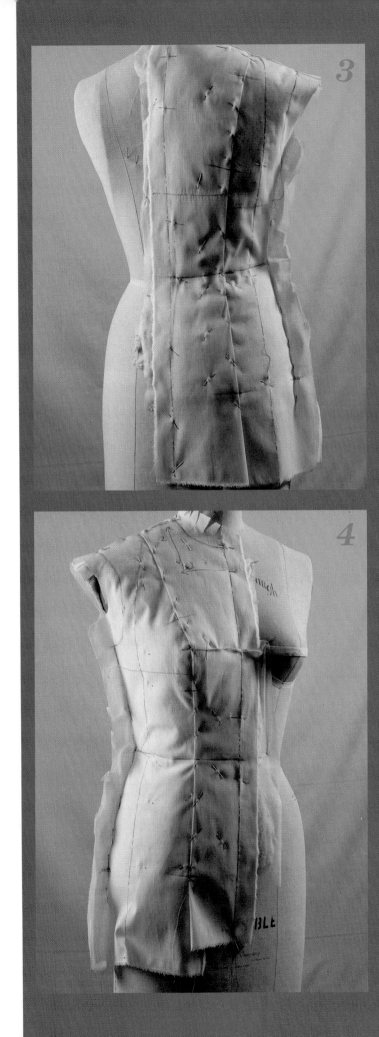

The finished drape

Here's the final stage of the draping. Every seam is pinned and marked (note that the side seams are pinned outward), neckline and armscye drawn. The muslin is ready to come off the form and be traced to paper.

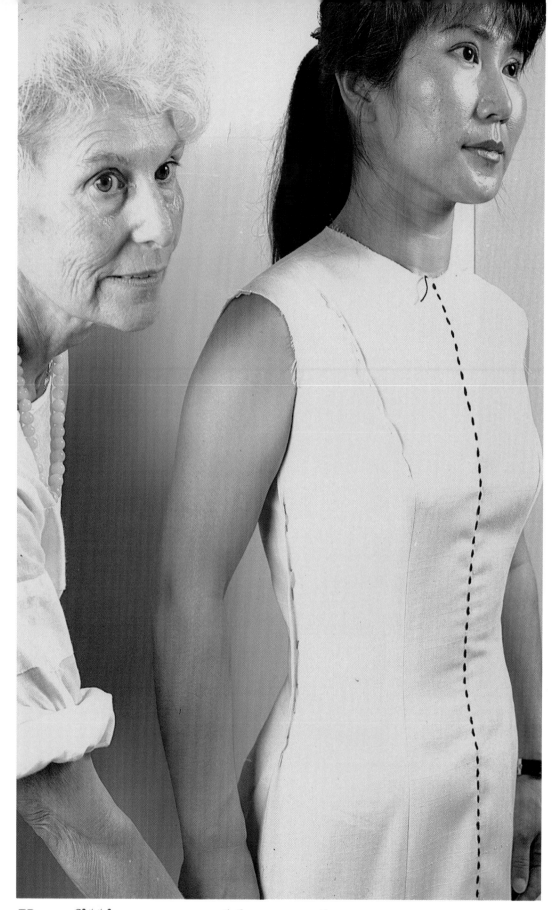

The Real You

A try-on is the only way to fit a muslin shell perfectly

by Suzanne Stern

Your fitting may not be complex

Suzanne Stern (left) has helped this student with her simple fitting problem (the muslin was loose at waist and between the bust and shoulders) by pinning the side seam and above the bust to reduce the circumference of the shell. Stern checks her work with a simple downward tug on the hem to simulate the weight of a real garment, which eliminates any resistant wrinkles.

no matter how you arrive at the final version of a fitting muslin, and no matter how you eventually plan to use it, the moment of truth is always the same: trying on the muslin and making the appropriate adjustments to fully customize it to a live body. Your two challenges are making sure that the seams and curves are positioned on the figure where you want them, and then adjusting the circumference of the shell to the degree of ease you want. As you'll see as you work on the muslin, sometimes you can deal with these issues separately, and sometimes you have to solve them at the same time.

I teach a class on couture draping in which each student drapes a muslin cover for a commercial dress form

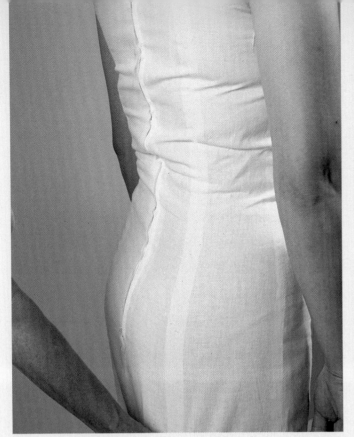 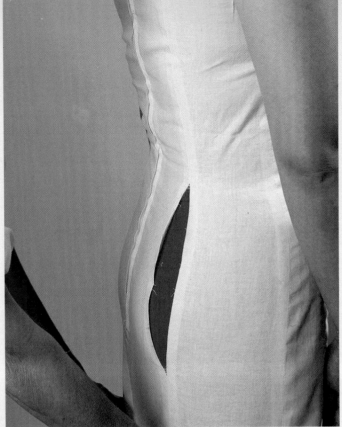

Too-tight hips can affect the bodice

Pull down on the hem to test the fit of the hips (left). If they're too tight, the entire bodice will look ill-fitting because it's being forced upwards. Once a seam is released below the waist to allow the waist to settle in place (right), the bodice corrects itself.

To correct the hips, balance the needed room right and left by opening a seam on the other side (top), but don't open a seam in front unless the front also needs extra room. Restitch the opened seams and try it on again.

padded to her individual shape, then fits the muslin snugly to her own figure, with my help. (This is the process I've been describing in other articles. See pp. 70-72 and pp. 73-76. *Ed. note:* Phone 800-888-8286 for back issues of *Threads.)* The photos here document the main parts of the fitting process I go through with my students. Even if you have not been following the padding steps up to now, you should be able to use many of these suggestions for perfecting any "skin-tight" fitting project, from a muslin sloper to a strapless gown.

If you *have* been following along, you should be at the stage described in the previous article, in which the seamlines of your initial drape have been trued and transferred to a paper pattern. Cut out the fitting version in the fabric you plan to use for the form cover, ideally something more durable than typi-

cal muslin. Some of my students didn't follow this advice and had to trace off their fitting muslins to cut the cover, which can lead to inaccuracies. Be sure to leave generous seam allowances (at least 1 in.) all around. Sew the cover on the seamlines with a long stitch, insert a full-length zipper in the center-back seam, and thread-trace (mark) the center-front line with a heavy contrasting thread. The person being fitted should wear the undergarments she normally prefers. Leave the seam allowances on the outside for easy access if you like, but I prefer to have them inside so it's easier to see the fit.

Start by balancing sides

Fitting, like the draping in the previous articles, is always done on the right half of the body in couture houses, but not before balancing both sides with one or two pins at several points on either side

of center front and back to keep those lines straight, vertical, and centered. Of course, this applies primarily if the shell fits loosely, which is the most likely problem.

If the shell is tight, you must release the appropriate seams and reshape them before balancing the sides. If the bust seems squashed, release the princess seams in front (or side seams in a darted shell). If the bodice is too tight, but the bust fit appears to be good, release the side seams. If the tension is at the midriff, you must decide where the excess flesh is and release the seams there. Often this means distributing the needed room among the princess and side seams. The photos above show how to check and correct a too-tight fit in the hips. Take the adjusted shell off and restitch the opened seams before proceeding.

To balance the shell, check first for differences between

left and right and eliminate them if possible. If one shoulder is higher, for example, fit the higher side, and then make both sides the same height when the fitting is complete, padding the lower shoulder to balance the final garment. Fitting the larger side and padding later can also correct for unsymmetrical breasts, but if one hip is higher, the waist must be tilted to reflect it, or else the skirt will never hang straight.

Next look over the general fit to see the problem spots. If the fit seems loose all over, start pinning the waist to fit by pinching out excess at the side seam, princess seams, or darts. Then start pinning out excess circumference along the side seam, without pulling the centers off. As you work, pull down on the hem occasionally, as I'm doing on p. 77, to see how a little weight, like that of a garment, will smooth out tiny wrinkles that you might otherwise spend unnecessary time trying to pin away.

Fitting the bust

Verify the placement of the bust point, adjusting if necessary by reshaping the princess seam or repositioning the dart, and pin the small horizontal dart from the points towards the center-front seam. I usually wait until this stage to place this dart,

because it usually needs correcting if done earlier, as was the case with the student in the photo on p. 80.

The most common area to need alteration at the bust is the complex curve from above the bust to the shoulder and over to the armscye. Shown directly below is a typical example of the fullness and wrinkles many people will find here. If you're fitting darts, you simply need to

open up the side-seam dart and re-form it until the section above the bust lies smoothly against the figure. Let the dart go wherever it wants to, and if a curve seems to be forming, let it curve. Remember that you're fitting skin-tight and don't need any ease here on a fitting shell.

If you're fitting a princess seam, start the alteration by opening the seam from shoulder almost to the bust point

and releasing the shoulder seam from the princess line to the armhole. Students are often tempted to simply pin the seam tighter, taking up the same amount of excess on each side. This doesn't work because the fitting problem is entirely in the side panel, and pinning this way curves and displaces the line of the seam. If the change needed is slight, you can sometimes simply fold and pin the side panel

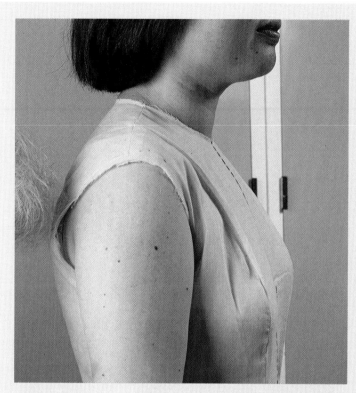

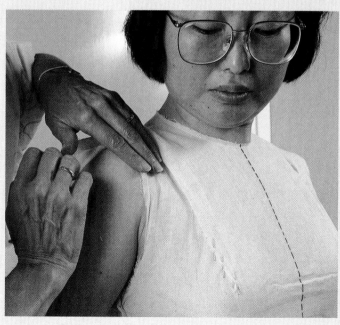

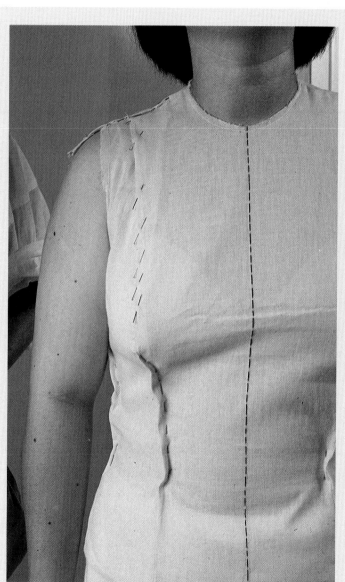

Fitting from bust to shoulder

To correct an ill-fitting side panel of a princess seam above the bust (top left photo), the most common fitting problem in the bust area, release the princess seam from the bust point to the shoulder seam, slide the side piece under the unaltered princess seam, and pin (photo at left). Below the bust in the photo above, you can pin the sides of the seam together to match the less-critical contour there.

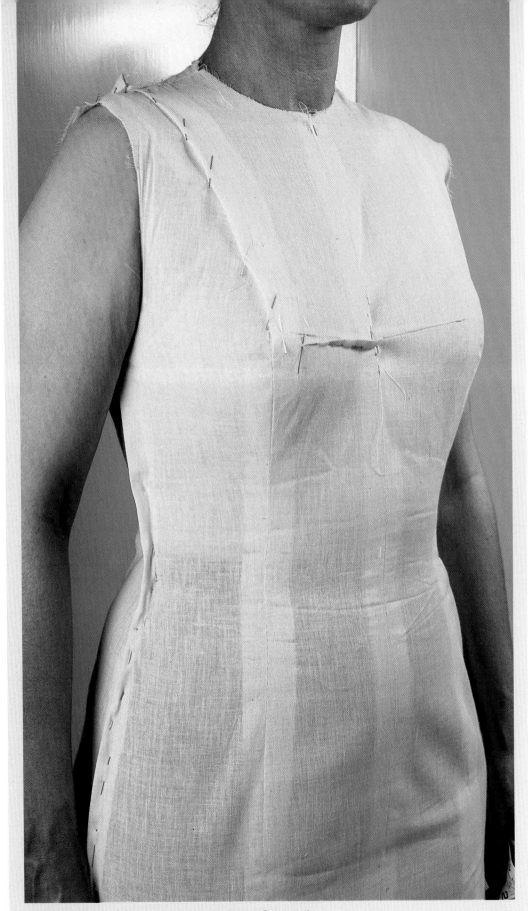

Contouring the center front

To shape the front to the curve between the bust points, pin a horizontal dart at bust level towards the center front. (Typically, fitting muslins don't have center-front seams.) Shown above is a good example of what a well-fitted muslin should look like.

under the front piece along the unopened seam, without changing the princess line, as I've done in the photo on p. 77. When you need more substantial changes, by opening the seam you can keep the front piece undisturbed and leave the princess line appearing straight.

Smooth the excess fabric of the side panel under the princess seam and pin it, as in the lower left-hand photo on p. 79. It's often not possible to completely pin away all the wrinkles, as you can see in the right-hand photo on p. 79, but if after you've done your best you pull sideways lightly on the raw edge of the armhole seam of the altered side panel, as an attached sleeve would pull, you'll see the last wrinkles disappear. Under the bust in this case I've pinned the princess seam closer to the figure by taking up the seam equally on both sides; the seam will still look straight even after you change its contour by pinning both sides.

Fitting the back

Unless the back is very rounded, you can get away with pinning the back princess seam smaller by taking up both sides evenly, as long as front and back princess seams still meet at the shoulder line. For a rounded back, you can open the seam from the shoulder down to the widest part and swing the back side panel underneath the center panel at the top to reduce the excess, as in the front.

If you are fitting someone who has a back waist with a deep inward curve and an exaggerated behind, as a dancer might, you probably need to remove the extra length at the center back. Pinch out a long horizontal dart along the waistline, starting at the center back and tapering away towards the side seam. This acts as a partial waistline seam.

Adding extra fabric

If you're missing fabric in spots, such as at the armhole if you've had to shift the side

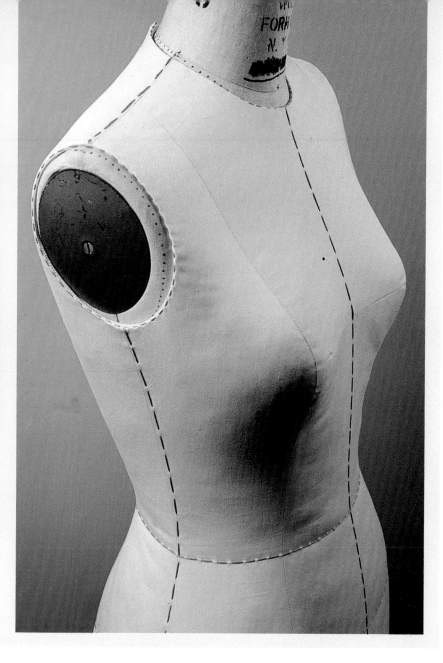

A finished cover

Thread-traced seams, centers, and waistline, plus facings and a center-back zipper (right) complete the dress-form-covering project. If your cover needs to be removable, protect the inside of the padding with fusible strips of non-woven interfacing (above).

panels toward the princess seams, you can piece in extra bits, but this is worth avoiding if possible by starting out with wide seam allowances. If you've no other recourse, don't try to make a regular seam. Instead, slip a piece of fabric flat under the raw edge that needs extending, matching grains carefully. Handstitch from the top through both layers, then trim raw edges. You can cover the seam with seam binding later to clean it up, if you like. The other alternative is to cut a new cover.

Finishing the cover

When you are satisfied with the fitting, hold your tape measure around the waist and mark along the bottom edge to show the true waist. When the cover is completed, you can thread-trace the marks to show the waistline permanently. The other important lines (except for the center front, which should already be thread-traced) are all marked with seams. You can thread-trace these too, as one student has done on the cover shown in the photo above, to make them easier to see and feel under other fabrics when you're using your form.

To finish the cover, take it off, mark both sides of each pinned change, and unpin them. Then replace all your pinned changes with thread tracing so you can transfer them to the other side of the cover. Fold the cover carefully in half along the center-front line with wrong sides together. Pin the seamlines on one side exactly on top of the same seams on the other side, then transfer the changes by sticking a pin through the thread tracing and marking the point where it emerges. Using your original pattern, draw and cut facing pieces for the cover's neckline and armscyes, and attach them after correcting the fit.

For the next step, you'll need to pad the other side of your form to match the padding described in the article on p. 70. You don't have to cover this second side with nonwoven fusible to hold it in place since it will be covered right away with your new fitted cover. When you think you're getting close, slip the cover onto the form with the facings out of the way on the right side and shift or add padding until the cover fits smoothly on both the right and left sides. When all is done to your satisfaction, slip the facings to the wrong side underneath the padding. Leave the zipper in back so you can take the cover off to alter for figure changes later on. □

Suzanne Stern teaches at Los Angeles Trade-Technical College, where her couture draping classes have long waiting lists.

When Draping Calls for Darts

If you want a close fit, several darts may work better than one seam

Draping to fit the full-busted figure presents special challenges. To show how two draping methods respond to the task, we've draped each side of a custom dress form using a different technique. On this page are the results of using two narrow pieces of tissue paper joined over the bust point with a single vertical seam, called a princess seam. On the facing page we used a single piece of tissue, and formed the shaping with three darts. The results are obvious: A single seam can't do the job. To learn how to drape an exact duplicate of the full figure using darts, read on.

From *Threads* magazine (June 1993) 47:58-61

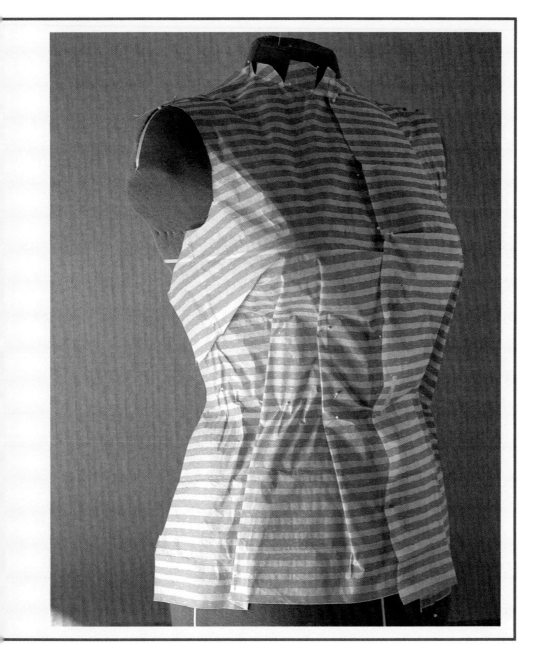

by Suzanne Pierrette Stern

Surprising as it may seem, it's often easier to fit the female figure with a single piece of fabric than with two pieces. In fact, the more shapely the figure, the more likely a single piece is to do the trick. This applies whenever you need to form-fit a large-busted figure. And it is true of the draping project that I've been describing in the previous few issues: reshaping a dress form to duplicate your figure.

To bring new readers up to speed, in a previous article (p. 73) I described the easiest technique for draping flat fabric around the contours of the average figure, which is to use a vertical seam from shoulder to hip that passes over the bust point. This is the familiar princess seam found on most dress forms and used extensively in formfitting garments.

But a quick glance at the photos at left will reveal what some of you, who have tried the princess-seam approach, have already discovered. If you're trying to fit a large bust, princess seams simply can't do it. You need the additional control that you can get only from darts. In this article, I'll describe how to use the basic principle of draping—*First place the grains, and then use the excess in seams, darts, or design lines*—to shape the muslin to your form with darts. The photos on the following pages show the procedure step by step.

Which method?

Darts work better whenever the fabric left after the grains are placed is more than the single seamline can remove. You could think of the princess seam as two

...from *Threads* magazine **83**

darts meeting at the bust point which have been converted to seams. But some figures need more than two darts. How do you know which method to use? If you're easy to fit in regular-size dresses, the princess line will do fine. If you have a hard time finding dresses that fit, and always have to alter patterns at the bust, use the dart method. It's appropriate for women with larger bustlines, regardless of whether their waists are small or ample.

It's important to remember that you're not draping a garment in this process, so you don't have to worry about style lines.

What you're doing is looking for the best way to fit the fabric to the shape, so use the steps here as guidelines, but let the conditions of *your* project take precedence. For instance, it's not necessary to drape the front and back using the same technique, so you can use a princess seam in back if you prefer. You only need darts in back when the figure is stooped, but I usually prefer to use the same method front and back. If you feel that an additional dart at any point would improve the fit, by all means use one. This applies equally to the princess-line drape;

if a dart would help any area of that project, insert one. Wherever they are, don't cut the darts, since they may need to be repositioned when you fit the muslin on your body.

Preparing the muslin for draping
Since there will be no seam over the bust or in back over the shoulder blade (if you use the dart method there, too), you will only need one piece of muslin for the front and one piece for the back. Estimate the length you'll need to cover the form from neck to hips, plus a few inch-

Draping a darted muslin

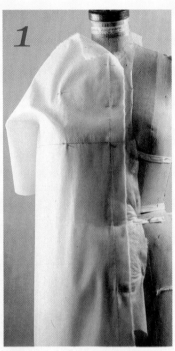

1 *Start by aligning the vertical pulled threads (marked with red thread for the photo) on the front piece with the form's CF, with the crossgrain threads level at the bustline, leaving 2 in. above the shoulder. Pin at the base of the neck on CF and about 3 in. below. Pin the crossgrain at the bust point and at the shoulder near the neck. Pin the CF at the waist and hip, allowing the muslin to follow the contour of the bust.*

2 *At the bust level at CF, fold out the excess into a dart, and pin it. Hold the crossgrain level at the bustline, and pin it under the armhole. This will create excess above the bust, but leave it there for now. Let the straight grain fall vertically between the side seam and the bust point, and pin it at the waist. Divide the excess under the bust into two darts, equidistant from the bust point and slightly below it. Pin all the way down below the waist, and off the edge if necessary. Then clip the neckline.*

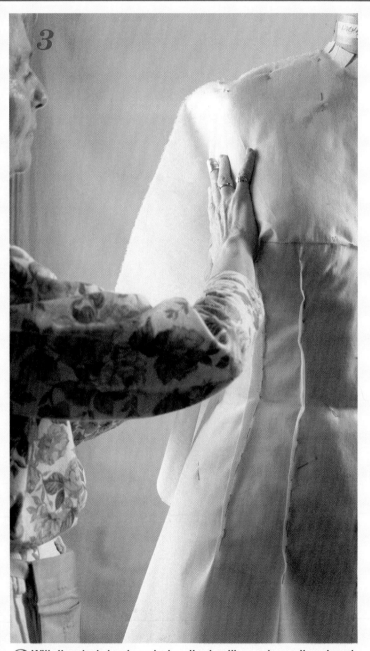

3 *With the darts in place below the bustline, release the pins at the side seam above the waist. Smooth the muslin along the crossgrain on the upper chest toward the bottom of the armhole and the end of the shoulder, and pin there.*

es, and tear the muslin to length. Separate it lengthwise in two equal pieces. Before pressing, pull two adjacent lengthwise threads 1 to 1¼ in. from the edge opposite the selvage on each piece (see *Threads* No. 45, p. 16). This will mark center back and center front. On the piece you'll use for the front, allow 2 in. above the shoulder, estimate where the bustpoint level is, and pull two crossgrain threads there. On the back piece do the same thing, but position the crossgrain at the shoulder-blade level. Press the pieces carefully, checking and correcting

the grain as needed. These basic muslin preparations are described in more detail in the article on pp. 73-76.

Marking the draped muslin

When you're satisfied with the drape, check everything and then mark each seamline and dart before taking the muslin off the form for patternmaking (described in the article on pp. 73-76). Outline side and shoulder seamlines on both sides and make cross marks at right angles to the seams to show how the sides fit together, like notches in a pattern.

Mark the end points of each dart first, then go down each side of the dart, running your marker along the fabric covering the pins that hold the dart in place. Draw in a temporary neckline and armscye, making each smaller than you think you'll need. These will be adjusted when you try on the full-body version of the muslin to check the fit. But that's in the article on pp. 77-81. ☐

Suzanne Pierrette Stern wrote about padding a dress form in Threads *No. 44, and draping in* Threads *No. 45.*

4 Shift excess downward and to the side seam, forming a curved dart ending in the side seam. Let it go where it wants, anywhere on the side seam. Sometimes it even works best going through the waistline. Pin the dart, then repin the side seam. Trim excess outside the side and shoulder seams, then move back the pins there and fold back the front muslin so you can work on the back. Leave 2 in. above the shoulder in back as in front, pinning straight grain on CB from base of the neck to the edge of the torso. Make sure you have plenty of fabric to go around the hips. Clip the neckline and pin

it near the shoulder. Smooth the crossgrain across the level of the shoulder blade or widest part of the upper back, and pin near the armhole. From there, smooth the straight grain up toward the shoulder.

5 Form the excess into a shoulder dart, on or near the princess line marked on the padding, more or less perpendicular to the shoulder line. Smooth the fabric down from the shoulder-blade level around the armhole, keeping grain fairly straight; pin at the side seam. Form the excess into two darts, ideally on each side of the princess line. Start pinning at the dart tips where the

excess begins and take them all the way down to the waist, then on to the hips. If the back is quite curved, you can sometimes improve the fit by moving the CB straight grain at the waistline sideways towards the undraped side up to ½ in. without shifting the grain at the hips and shoulder blades. This creates a shaped CB seamline.

6 Adjust the side seams and pin front and back together, allowances to the outside as shown, then fold the front shoulder seam over the back. Mark and trim as before.

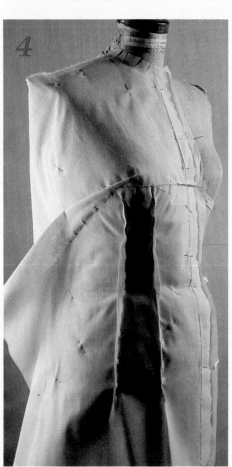

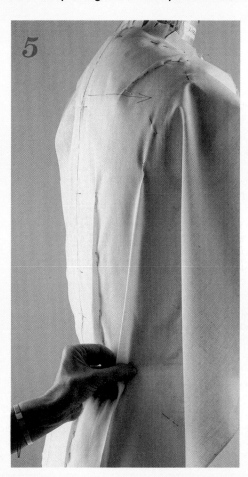

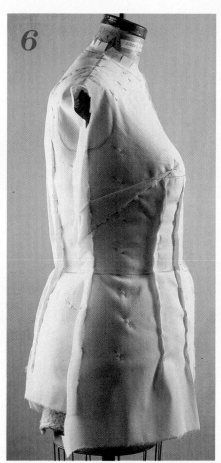

Making Room for Waists

If the hips fit, most skirts or pants can be easily expanded to fit in the waist, too

by Melissa Ingling-Leath

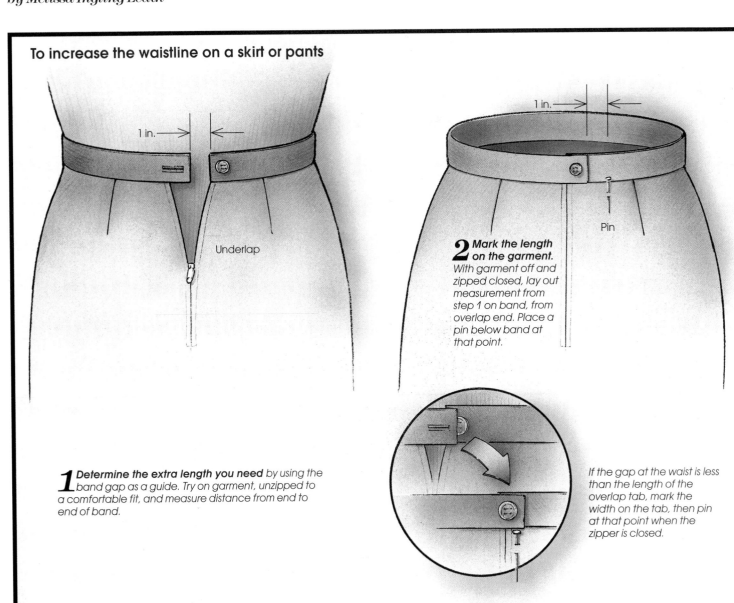

To increase the waistline on a skirt or pants

1 in.

Underlap

1 **Determine the extra length you need** by using the band gap as a guide. Try on garment, unzipped to a comfortable fit, and measure distance from end to end of band.

1 in.

Pin

2 **Mark the length on the garment.** With garment off and zipped closed, lay out measurement from step 1 on band, from overlap end. Place a pin below band at that point.

If the gap at the waist is less than the length of the overlap tab, mark the width on the tab, then pin at that point when the zipper is closed.

just about the commonest problem most of us have with ready-to-wear skirts or pants that *almost* fit is that the waistband is too snug. Expanding the waistline is certainly among the most frequent jobs I do working in the alteration department of a dress shop. Happily, as long as the hips fit well, expanding the waistline has one of the most straightforward solutions of all the problems I fix.

You'll need to almost completely remove the waistband, but once that's done, you can usually get three or even four extra inches out of the garment at the waist. You can get the extra material from the ease built into the waist seam (typically about 1 to 1½ in.), by stealing from any gathers or pleats, and as a last resort by opening up and restitching the darts and/or the side seams. If the garment hasn't been worn or cleaned often,

these seamlines usually can be pressed open without revealing the original stitching line.

The basic procedure has three main steps. First you measure the amount of extra length you need with the garment on and unzipped to the level of a comfortable fit, and remove the band by ripping the seam (see *Basics, Threads* No. 47, p. 24, for more on seam ripping). Then you expand the body of the garment using one or more of the additional fabric sources just described, and finally you extend and reattach the band, adding the extra to the underlap, or button end. If it's critical that the patch be invisible, you can look for matching fabric at the hem, from the wrong side of the waistband, and sometimes from inside the pockets. Make sure you match the grain of the band with your patch material. If you'll always be wearing a belt with the garment, or will wear sweaters over the

waist, you may not mind using a matching lining fabric; check fabric-store remnant tables for a scrap in the right color.

The drawings below show the process step by step. Since you can't tell exactly how much length you'll have to steal from pleats, darts, or seams until you've got the band off and have pressed out the ease, you simply mark the amount of change you need on the garment with a pin (see step 2), and check the unextended band against the mark after you press out the ease (step 4). Divide the remaining needed amount between the other sources. You can make an estimate before you start by stretching out the ease (or any gathers) just below the band, and by checking the width of darts, pleat underlayers, and seam allowances. □

Melissa Ingling-Leath makes one-of-a-kind garments and teaches alteration in Springfield, OH.

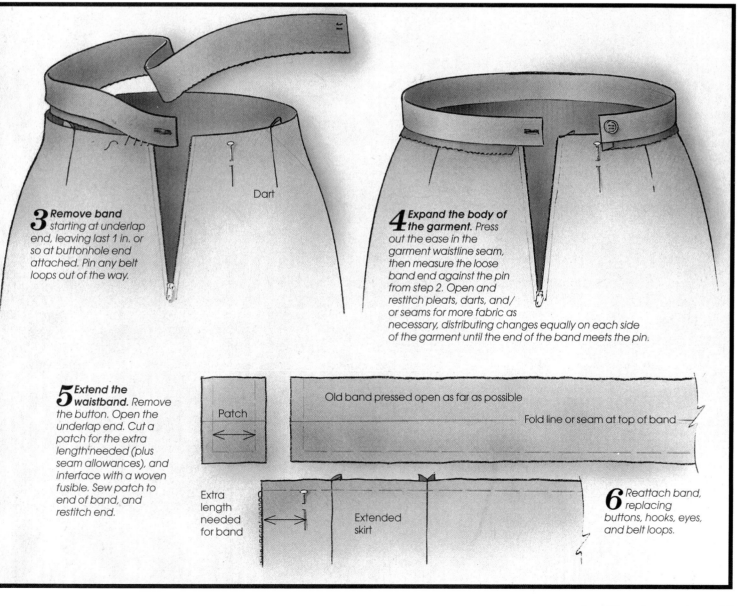

3 **Remove band** starting at underlap end, leaving last 1 in. or so at buttonhole end attached. Pin any belt loops out of the way.

Dart

4 **Expand the body of the garment.** Press out the ease in the garment waistline seam, then measure the loose band end against the pin from step 2. Open and restitch pleats, darts, and/or seams for more fabric as necessary, distributing changes equally on each side of the garment until the end of the band meets the pin.

5 **Extend the waistband.** Remove the button. Open the underlap end. Cut a patch for the extra length needed (plus seam allowances), and interface with a woven fusible. Sew patch to end of band, and restitch end.

Patch

Extra length needed for band

Old band pressed open as far as possible

Fold line or seam at top of band

Extended skirt

6 Reattach band, replacing buttons, hooks, eyes, and belt loops.

1 *Determine the amount of adjustment needed: Try on the garment, pinch to the correct fit, and pin. Measure from the fold to the pin using a seam gauge as shown (see Basics, Threads No. 48, for an introduction to seam gauges), and multiply the measure by 2. This is the amount to take in.*

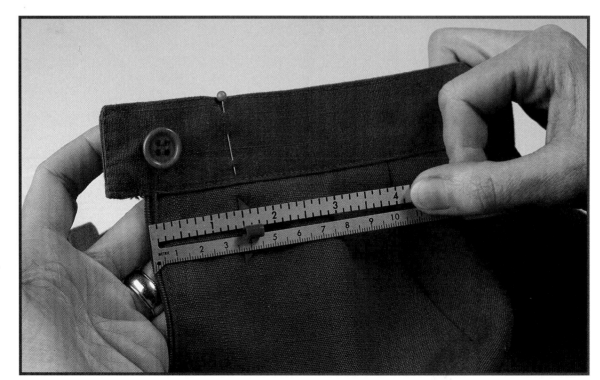

2 *Mark the adjustment on the garment: Starting at the right-side zipper teeth, mark the measurement with a pin on the waistband. This pin will match up with the zipper teeth after the garment body is altered.*

Taking in a Waistband

If the hips fit, you can easily alter the waist of pants or skirts to fit, too

by Melissa Ingling-Leath

few of us fit into a standard size store-bought skirt or pair of pants. Often, the size that fits nicely in the hips and crotch is too big in the waist. The good news is that taking in the waist of a garment is easy. After almost completely removing the waistband, you either gather the waist of the garment or make each dart and seam a little wider to remove the needed amount, following the steps shown here. For example, if you want to remove 1½ in. total from a garment's two front darts, two back darts, and two side seams, you'll take ¼ in. from each location. Each new stitching

line will be ⅛ in. from the old seamline. After replacing the waistband, you'll be well-rewarded with a waist that fits!

When sewing alterations, the goal is to leave the garment looking just as it did before it was altered (but with a better fit). Proper pressing will help you achieve this goal. Be sure to iron any new seams and darts after stitching. When you reattach the waistband, press the seam allowance up into the waistband before stitching the inner layer in place. □

Melissa Ingling-Leath teaches alteration in Springfield, OH. Her article about expanding a waistband to fit appears on pp. 86-87.

4 ***Remove the extra width from the waistline of the garment*** *by dividing the adjustment between darts, seams, and/or pleats and restitching them a little wider, as shown above. The pin marks the new stitching line. Stitch the new seam or dart before ripping out the old line of stitching, which keeps the seamlines aligned and allows you to measure the new stitching from the old seamline. Or you can gather along the waist seamline with long machine stitches, pull the bobbin thread until the waistband pin aligns with the zipper teeth, and distribute the gathers evenly around the waist.*

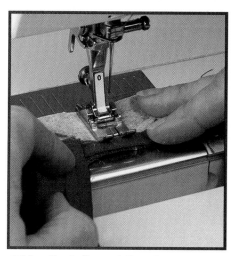

5 ***Reattach the waistband:*** *Place outside of waistband right sides together with garment body, aligning waistband pin with zipper teeth and matching stitching lines of band and garment. Stitch.*

Turn button end of waistband right sides together (place a pin to mark the top fold line) and stitch across the end to remove the extra length, as shown above. Trim, turn, and press the new end seam. Then attach the inside of the waistband to the garment by topstitching, or stitching in the ditch of the seamline, from the right side of the garment. Include the extension. Replace buttons, hooks, and belt loops.

3 ***Remove band,*** *leaving 1 in. or so attached at the buttonhole end (see Threads No. 47, p. 24 for information on ripping a seam). Remove all hooks, eyes, and buttons; pin any belt loops to the garment to mark their positions.*

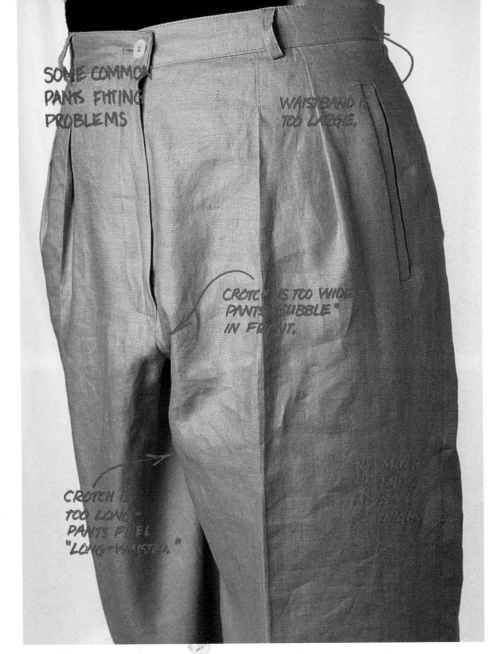

SOME COMMON PANTS FITTING PROBLEMS

WAISTBAND IS TOO LARGE.

CROTCH IS TOO WIDE PANTS "BUBBLE" IN FRONT.

CROTCH IS TOO LONG PANTS FEEL "LONG-WAISTED."

These Pants are Made for Striding

Altering to fit from navel to knees

by Mary A. Roehr

We've all tried on pants that didn't fit in the seat, or that felt tight or baggy across the thighs or in the crotch, like the linen pants in the photo at left. Traditionally, the fit in these three areas has been a mystery to many sewers. In fact, the stride—the area in the back of the thighs between the seat and the knees—is often either overlooked or ignored because it is so perplexing from an alteration standpoint. However, with the information that follows and a basic knowledge of sewing, you'll be able to alter the waist, seat, stride, and crotch to fit.

Men's and women's pants alterations require different approaches to fitting problems. Men are generally easier to fit than women because their body lines are more angular while women's are curved. Men's clothing is made with extra-large seam allowances to allow for alteration, while women's clothing rarely allows even ½-in. seams.

Waist and seat alterations

Working from the top down is a basic principle of fitting, since what is sewn above will affect the fit of the areas below. If the wearer's pants are too tight or too baggy in the seat and stride, first check to see if the waist is too tight or loose, because quite often a waist alteration will be needed at the same time you adjust the seat and stride. If the waist needs to be altered, mark it before you mark the seat and stride.

Check the waist by positioning the wearer in front of a mirror so you can see how the changes you make in the back affect the front of the pants. If the pants need taking in, grasp the excess material at the center back of the waist and secure it with a pin. Continue to pin down into the seat as far as needed (left-hand photo on facing page), but not past the point where the center-back seam begins to curve under the buttocks (this area will be addressed in the stride alteration). If the waistband is too thick to pin through, make chalk marks on each side of the ridge of excess fabric. Tailors rarely use pins for marking, but when they do, they usually mark over the pins with chalk. Then if the pins fall out, the marks won't be lost.

Marking the waist for letting out can be done in two different ways. I prefer to have the wearer unzip the pants as far as there is strain and then measure the amount of gap. By doing this, you can tell how far down into the seat the pants need to be let out. If you're uncomfortable with this method, measure the wear-

From *Threads* magazine (December 1991) 38:68-71

er's waist and let out the pants waist tapering the new sewing line down to nothing where the need for alteration ends. With this second method, you may need another fitting to see if you have sewn the proper distance into the seat.

Women's pants sometimes present waist altering problems. While men's pants almost always have a seam in the center back of the waistband (and are cut in such a way that all waist alterations are meant to be done in the center back), women's pants seldom do. If the waist needs to be taken in, you can remove the waistband only in the center back, cut it, and make a seam there. This facilitates letting out the waist again, should it become necessary. If you prefer to keep the waistband unbroken, you'll need to remove it completely (see the instructions on p. 92) and shorten it at the overlap.

Sometimes taking in the waist at the center back is not the best option for women's pants. If pinning out the excess in the back pulls the side seams backward and causes the creases to hang poorly, it could be that the front of the pants needs alteration as well as the back. In this case, remove the waistband and take in the pants at the side seams, or distribute the alteration among the two side seams and the center back.

For letting out the waist, you can sometimes find enough extra matching fabric in the hem to add to the waistband. Either add this piece to the overlap at the zipper, or set in a piece in the center back of the waistband.

Stride alterations in men's pants— Once you have marked the waist and seat, you can turn your attention to the stride. The stride is a standard alteration for men's pants and is almost always corrected by adjusting the back of the pants leg at the inseam. Taking in or letting out the *back crotch point* of the pants changes the circumference of the pants leg and the width of the bottom of the crotch.

If the stride needs to be taken in, there will be bagginess in the back of the thighs. If the waist needs altering, pin the waistband or hold it together while measuring the stride adjustment. Next, take a horizontal pinch of fabric from the center-back seam as shown in the far right photo above. Pinch out and pin enough fabric so the seam does not hang loosely on the seat. The amount of extra ease you pinch up here tells you how much fabric to take off the back crotch point. Mark the width of the pinch with chalk, and remove the pin.

Measure the amount of the pinch and take in the stride by this amount. On the

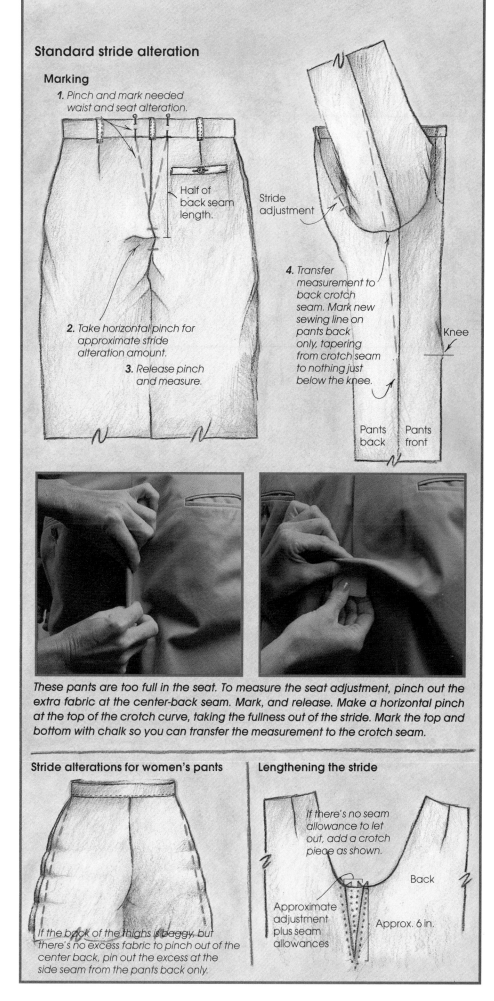

Standard stride alteration

Marking

1. Pinch and mark needed waist and seat alteration.

Half of back seam length.

Stride adjustment

2. Take horizontal pinch for approximate stride alteration amount.

3. Release pinch and measure.

4. Transfer measurement to back crotch seam. Mark new sewing line on pants back only, tapering from crotch seam to nothing just below the knee.

Knee

Pants back   Pants front

These pants are too full in the seat. To measure the seat adjustment, pinch out the extra fabric at the center-back seam. Mark, and release. Make a horizontal pinch at the top of the crotch curve, taking the fullness out of the stride. Mark the top and bottom with chalk so you can transfer the measurement to the crotch seam.

Stride alterations for women's pants

If the back of the thighs is baggy, but there's no excess fabric to pinch out of the center back, pin out the excess at the side seam from the pants back only.

Lengthening the stride

If there's no seam allowance to let out, add a crotch piece as shown.

Back

Approximate adjustment plus seam allowances

Approx. 6 in.

outside of the pants back, mark the amount on the crotch seam and taper to nothing just below the knee (shown in the top right drawing on p. 91). This removes the extra fabric from the back of the thighs and alters the stride.

When the stride needs to be let out, the pants will pull in the back of the thighs. It is difficult to determine how much to let the stride out because there is no way to measure this. I have learned from experience that the amount the waist is let out will determine how much the stride needs to be let out. In general, if the waist is let out 1 to 1½ in., I would let the stride out about 1 in. If the waist and seat were let out more than 1½ in. and the stride looked very tight, I would let it out about 1¾ in. to 2 in.

If the waist, seat, and stride all need to be altered, rip out the lower crotch seam and the leg seam. Remove or add the amount marked from the back inseam only. Take in or let out the waist and seat as marked, closing the lower crotch seam at the same time. If you remove more than 1½ in., trim the seam allowance to 1 in. Altering the stride will cause the back crease to move inward, so you must lay the pants out and press in a new crease from just below the knee up.

Altering the stride in women's pants— Because women's bodies have so many variations (with rounded hips, flat seats, and thin thighs), the stride alteration described above may not work. There are alternatives, however.

When there is bagginess in the back of the thighs, but you can't pinch excess fabric horizontally from the center-back seam (as in marking for the stride), it means that the extra fabric was cut on the sides of the pants. Pin out the fullness at the outseam from the back, and remove it from the back of the legs only (drawing at bottom left, p. 91), not equally on the front and back.

If the wearer has a very flat seat and there is a lot of bagginess in the seat and stride, you may also have to lower the back waistband. Pin out the excess fabric on the sides of the pants as described above, and make a tuck below the waistband, as shown in the top drawing on the facing page, until the back of the pants is smooth. Mark the alterations. Release the waistband and restitch it to the pants back along the marked line.

If the pants pull across the back of the thighs, the stride needs to be let out. Since there is rarely extra fabric at the inseam in women's pants, adding a crotch piece may be the only way to alter a tight stride. A crotch piece is a triangular fab-

ric gusset, usually about 6 in. long, and as wide at the top as needed. Of course, a crotch piece can only be added if there is matching fabric available. If you did not make the pants and there are no scraps, sometimes you can cut a piece from the hem and face the hem.

Cut the crotch piece wider than you think the stride adjustment needs to be so you can experiment with the fit. Insert the crotch piece into the inseam as shown in the bottom right drawing on p. 91, and then resew.

If a crotch piece is impossible or unacceptable, you may not be able to correct the problem.

Altering the crotch

Crotch fit is a separate issue, usually not related to the alterations discussed above. The waist and the crotch may need altering at the same time, but in my experience this is rare. Because of the differences in weight distribution of men and women, men tend to have problems with the *width* of the crotch, while women more often have problems with the crotch *length*. The difference is illustrated at the bottom of the facing page.

Baggy crotch in men's pants—When the crotch is too loose in men's pants, the fabric may form loose wrinkles at the bottom of the fly. A man will usually complain that the pants "bubble out" or that there is "too much fabric in the crotch area."

You can correct this by pinning out the extra fabric on the front inseams only. If you are uncomfortable doing this, you can make a mental estimate of the amount to be taken in (usually ¼ in. to ⅜ in.), and pin the seams after the pants have been removed. Then the wearer can slip them on to check the fit. For sewing, rip open the bottom of the crotch curve and the inseam about halfway to the knee. Resew the inseams first, taking in the necessary amount on the front only. This reduces the width of the crotch curve. Resew the crotch seam.

Long crotch in women's pants—For women's pants, the crotch is usually too long if the pants feel baggy in the crotch or they are too long-waisted. Usually you will need to lower the waistband to pull the crotch up all the way around, but occasionally only the front or back will need the alteration. For marking, pin out a fold of fabric around the waistband as needed until the crotch area appears or feels comfortable, as shown at top, facing page. Measure the amount pinned and mark the new sewing line below the

waistband. If only the front or back of the waistband needs to be dropped, taper the new sewing line to nothing a few inches past the side seams.

Remove the waistband and be sure to mark where it was attached at the center front, center back, and side seams. In pants with a zipper, lowering the waistband means that you will have to take the zipper into account. If the amount of adjustment is less than 1 in., you can just cut off the excess zipper, being careful to cut between the teeth. An alteration of an inch or more means you will have to move the zipper down as shown in the drawing at center, facing page, before reapplying the waistband.

When resewing the waistband, remember that the pants waist should be at least ½ in. larger in circumference than the waistband. This extra must be eased in and will contribute to a proper fit. Baste on the new sewing line to help the easing process. If there is more than 1 in. of ease, narrow the waist by taking in the side seams.

Crotch too tight—On both men's and women's pants, there will be pull lines radiating from the crotch area when the crotch is too tight. The ideal way to correct the problem would be to raise the waistband on women's pants (thus increasing the crotch length), and to let out the front inseam on men's pants (thus increasing the crotch width). Unfortunately, there is frequently not enough fabric for these procedures.

With women's pants, cutting the crotch curve deeper and restitching it will sometimes help, although this cannot be done more than ½ in. without adversely affecting the fit of the seat and thighs. Do it in ¼-in. increments, and most importantly, draw a smoothly curved new crotch line, as shown in the bottom drawing, facing page. The crotch curve in both men's and women's pants should resemble a U-shape, and even slight deviation from a smooth line can be felt by the wearer. Trimming the seam allowance to ¼ in. in the very bottom of the crotch curve will provide the most comfortable fit.

To alleviate a tight crotch in men's pants, try to let out the front inseam, reversing the alteration procedure for a baggy crotch. Since it is difficult to fit this area, you can get an idea of how much to let out by asking the wearer if the crotch is slightly tight or very tight. If he replies, "Just a little tight," it probably needs to be let out ¼ in. to ½ in.

If the crotch is very tight, indicating the need for more than ½ in. extra fabric, you may let some out of the back inseam too, but not more than 1 in. total, or the seat and stride will be affected. Let the seams out, tapering to nothing about 4 in. below the crotch. Sew the new seams twice since the crotch is a high-stress area.

For both men and women, if the wearer has gained weight (usually 10 pounds or more), wants extra fabric in the crotch to provide more ease of movement (such as in sportswear), or has a worn area in the crotch, you can sometimes add a crotch piece.

Binding in the crotch—A final crotch alteration calls for reshaping the crotch seam, usually in the back of the pants. This is needed when the pants fit well except for a binding between the buttocks in the lower seat area. The wearer will probably complain of being able to feel the pants in the seat. This means that the lower seat curve is not U-shaped enough to correspond to the shape of the wearer's body.

First make a mark on the outside of the pants at the exact spot of discomfort. Then lay the crotch seam flat so you can see the whole curve, front and back. You can slip one leg of the pants into the other to help you see the curve. Usually the seat curve will be cutting up between the buttocks at too sharp an angle, which causes the binding. Remembering that, in general, the ideal crotch curve is in the shape of a smooth U, look at the problem area and decide what you can do to improve it. Reshape the crotch curve 1/8 in. at a time until it fits. Use sharpened tailors' chalk and experiment with drawing new seat curves using your mark as a point of reference.

Changing the curve as little as 1/8 in. and not more than 3/8 in. will make a big difference in the feel of the pants. Stretch the seam as you sew the new crotch curve so the stitching will be less likely to break under stress. After checking the fit, trim the seam following the new curve.

Doing alterations is largely a process of trial and error, and your expertise will build as your experience grows. Pants are definitely the most difficult garment to fit, but the more you work with them, the more you will learn. □

Mary Roehr has operated a custom tailoring business for 15 years and has written four books on the subject, including Altering Women's Ready-to-Wear *and* Altering Men's Ready-to-Wear, *available from Mary Roehr Custom Tailoring, 3597 Vicksburg Ct., Tallahassee, FL, 32308.*

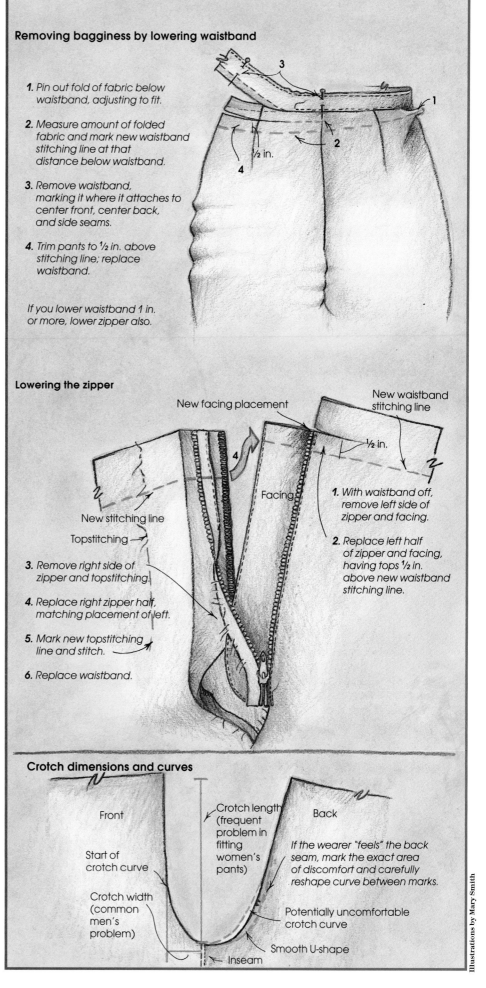

Removing bagginess by lowering waistband

1. Pin out fold of fabric below waistband, adjusting to fit.

2. Measure amount of folded fabric and mark new waistband stitching line at that distance below waistband.

3. Remove waistband, marking it where it attaches to center front, center back, and side seams.

4. Trim pants to 1/2 in. above stitching line; replace waistband.

If you lower waistband 1 in. or more, lower zipper also.

1/2 in.

Lowering the zipper

New facing placement

New waistband stitching line

1/2 in.

New stitching line

Topstitching

Facing

1. With waistband off, remove left side of zipper and facing.

2. Replace left half of zipper and facing, having tops 1/2 in. above new waistband stitching line.

3. Remove right side of zipper and topstitching.

4. Replace right zipper half, matching placement of left.

5. Mark new topstitching line and stitch.

6. Replace waistband.

Crotch dimensions and curves

Front

Crotch length (frequent problem in fitting women's pants)

Back

Start of crotch curve

If the wearer "feels" the back seam, mark the exact area of discomfort and carefully reshape curve between marks.

Crotch width (common men's problem)

Potentially uncomfortable crotch curve

Smooth U-shape

Inseam

Illustrations by Mary Smith

Index